Why Me?

Navigating the Unbearable Truth of Grief and Loss

VERIFICATION OF CERTIFICATION

This is to verify official Certification of

SHIRLEY JOHNSON

as a Certified Grief Counselor, by the American Academy of Grief Counseling. This certified member may use the initials GC-C, in professional recognition of achieved certification. This certification is given upon the successful fulfillment of all requirements for such, as established and approved by the Governing Board and Advisory Board.

by

Shirley Tripp Johnson, GC-C

© 2025 Shirley Tripp Johnson.
All Rights Reserved

"Photography by Christopher Meder"

Illustration by: Shirley Tripp Johnson, GC-C

Dedications

In Loving Memory
Tripp "TrippNAintEZ" Taylor
10/5/82 – 2/17/10

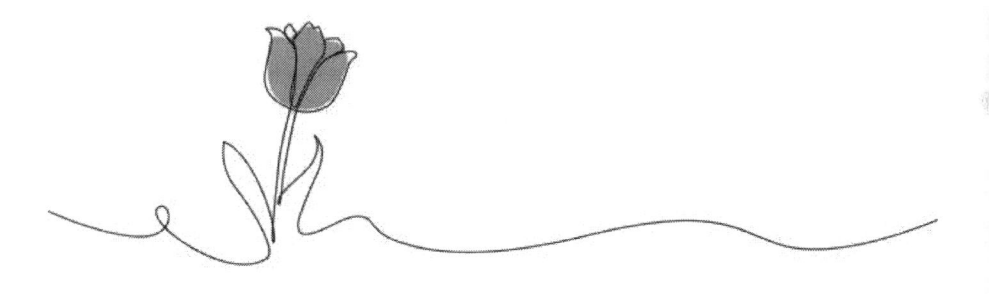

—To my husband, Dan, my daughter, Deidre, and my son, Jeremiah—
You saved my life without even knowing it.
In my darkest moments, your love was my light.

_ Thank you, Melanie Marshall, for dedicating your time to reading *Why Me?* and offering thoughtful input on editing improvements.

A Heart-Felt Message

To all of you I have gotten very close to. You know who you are.

You've been my anchors in rough waters, my laughter through the chaos, and my constant reminder that joy can always be found, no matter the circumstances.

Your support has been a light in the dark through the tough times. Whether it was a kind word, a shared laugh, or simply your presence, you've reminded me I'm never alone. And in the fun times, you've shown me how to fully embrace life, finding happiness in the little things and big moments.

I'm endlessly grateful for each of you—for the love, laughter, and memories we've created together. I truly wouldn't have made it through without you, and I can't wait to see what adventures and joys lie ahead for us.

Thank you for being the incredible people you are and for sharing your heart with me. You're more than friends; you're family. I love you all so much.

With all my heart,

Shirley

Table of Contents

Chapter 1 - The Stages of Grief - Need Not Apply 5

Chapter 2 - Tragedy Strikes 11

Chapter 3 - My Broken Heart is Never Going to Heal 27

Chapter - 4 Grief Speaks 41

Chapter - 5 Shattered by Grief 59

Chapter 6 - Finding My Way Back to Joy 73

Chapter 7 - Rebuilding Through Brokenness 87

Chapter 8 - Connecting with Fellow Grievers 97

Chapter 9 -
Random Thoughts and Emotions through the years 107

Chapter 10 - Grace Through Grief 127

Chapter 11 - Headlines of Heartbreak 133

Personal Anecdotes

Polly Groves: On May 6, 2011, my life changed forever. I lost my only child in a fatal car accident. He was just 20 years old. At that moment, it felt like my entire world had ended. My family encouraged me to seek grief counseling immediately, but I wasn't ready. The pain was overwhelming, and I couldn't bring myself to talk about it. After a few months, I quit going.

Six months after the accident, I was scrolling through Facebook when I thought, *there has to be something for people like me—mothers who've lost a child.* I began searching and came across *Wings of Hope: Living Forward After the Loss of a Child.* Without hesitation, I signed up.

That decision changed everything. Almost immediately, mothers from the group began reaching out to me, and I finally felt like I could share my story. Shirley was one of the first to call me. She spoke with such warmth and understanding that it felt like she truly *got it.* In those early days, when I could barely see a way forward, Shirley became a lifeline. She listened without judgment, let me cry, and reminded me that I wasn't alone.

It wasn't just her words—it was her heart. Shirley seemed to know exactly what I needed, even when I didn't. She gently encouraged me to keep going, even when all I wanted was to give up. I can't count the number of times I called her, completely overwhelmed, and she patiently talked me through my pain. Her kindness helped me take the small steps I needed to start healing.

Six years after joining Wings of Hope, Shirley convinced me to attend my first retreat. I was terrified—nervous about walking into a room full of strangers and unsure of what to expect. But Shirley assured me it would be okay. "Just come," she said. "We'll be there for you."

When I arrived, I was embraced with open arms. Everyone was so welcoming, and for the first time, I was surrounded by people who truly understood what I was feeling. That week was life-changing. I healed in ways I never thought possible, and it was Shirley who kept me grounded through it all. She checked on me constantly, making sure I was okay and encouraging me to share my story.

Since then, I've attended every retreat I could. A few years later, I even brought my husband to a family retreat. Shirley was right there, helping him navigate the complexities of grief and showing him how to support me. She taught him that he wasn't just helping me heal; we were healing together.

Shirley has become so much more than a friend—she's like family. She's the person I call when the grief feels unbearable, the one who always seems to have the right words to pull me back from the edge. Her unwavering support has been a constant light on this long and difficult journey.

Wings of Hope and the incredible people I've met through it, especially Shirley, have given me the strength to keep moving forward. This road of grief is never-ending, but with Shirley by my side and the connections I've made along the way, I know I'll never have to walk it alone.

Barbara Dykes: The Wings of Hope Retreats truly saved my life. The incredible moms and dads I've met through these retreats have been my lifeline during some of the hardest days. You've become like family to me, filling the emptiness I felt when I thought I was completely lost and alone.

Finding this group and attending the retreats was the turning point in my healing journey. That's when I began to see a way forward. Shirley, I can't thank you enough for your kindness and guidance. And to everyone I've met through Wings of Hope, thank you from the bottom of my heart. I love you all more than words can say.

Donna Coster: Traveling this road with Shirley Tripp-Johnson and all our incredible friends has made it bearable. I honestly can't imagine my life without each of you. This journey is one none of us ever wished to take, but I'm so grateful to have you by my side.

One of the most healing parts of my grief journey has been meeting and connecting with other parents who have experienced the loss of a child. I've learned that unless you've faced this unimaginable pain, it's impossible to truly understand it.

Attending retreats with other parents who share this loss has been profoundly comforting. We've found a space where our grief is understood, and our emotions are shared without judgment. Many of us have become close friends, and those friendships have been a lifeline.

On our worst days, we cry together, and on our better days, we celebrate moments of joy. I am so grateful for my Angel Moms. I love you all deeply.

Shirley, thank you for everything you've done for us. Your love, strength, and kindness have been a guiding light. I love you with all my heart and soul.

Iva Jean Tennant

Hugs and love

Lifesavers for sure— I so miss the retreats

Rhonda Sykes

This group of strangers that became friends and now forever family saved my life! I now have friends/family for life. I will forever be grateful to this group. You all know who you are! Love you all!

Sharon Wayman

It's a God send. Just having someone to talk to who understands the loss of a child has helped me live.

Lauri L Payne Daubert

(((Hugs))) Sincere heartfelt hugs...

I remember my first post to this group. I read several posts before I attempted it. To know... I was not alone in my grief, and that I had somewhere to cry out to other moms was a true God send. I thought I was crazy. I was not. I was a broken, grieving mom.

FOREWORD

As the author's daughter, I am honored to introduce this profound work. Grief is not simply the absence of someone you love—it is the loss of who you were before they left. It is the shattering of the life you knew, the fracture between what was and what will never be again. When my brother died, I lost more than my brother and friend. I lost my mother as I had always known her—she remained physically present, but sorrow consumed her essence. Our home, once full of laughter and familiarity, became unrecognizable. The world moved on, but for us, it had stopped.

I was pregnant with my third child when he died. Life and death existed within me at the same time—one heartbeat growing, another gone forever. No one prepares you for such a collision of emotions, for the impossible task of celebrating new life and coping with the devastation of loss in the same breath.

When I read my mother's words in *Why Me*, I didn't feel something new—I felt what I have always felt. My grief remains as raw as the day he left. But in her grief, I saw my own. We mourned the same person but grieved in different languages, walking separate yet intertwined paths of sorrow. This book does not offer resolution because grief has none. It does not fade; it only changes form. It threads within the marrow of your bones, shifting the weight of your presence, the cadence of your breath, and the way you inhabit time. It bends the light in your eyes and reshapes the way you love—not with the innocence of permanence, but with the aching knowledge life can abruptly vanish.

People speak of grief as a journey with an endpoint, a sequence of stages leading toward acceptance. But my mother reveals a deeper truth: grief is a staircase without a final step. You climb, believing you are rising above the pain, only to find yourself back in its grasp, forever ascending yet never arriving. This book will not heal you but bring your pain to the surface—not to erase it, but to make it known—

until you no longer resist its presence but learn to carry it as part of who you are.

My mother's grief is unimaginable, yet in these pages, she makes it tangible. She does not soften the edges or offer truisms. She lays it bare, exposing the unfiltered truth of the agony of losing a child. *Why Me* is not simply a story of loss—it is a testament to survival, to transformation when the unbearable force of love has nowhere to go.

If you are holding this book, it is likely because you, too, have lost someone inseparable from your existence. And for that, I am deeply sorry. No words nor wisdom can ease the ache. What you carry will never disappear, and I hope it doesn't—because that would mean losing the love, the memories, the invisible threads connecting you to them. Their presence lingers in every moment, a testament that they mattered, that they still do. But you are here, still breathing, still moving forward—not despite the heaviness, but because you forged a strength-defying reason, a resilience born from love, loss, and the unwavering will to carry both. And that is an extraordinary act of courage.

Deidre

FOREWORD

I first learned about Why Me? when my mom sent me a text message that said, "...I wrote a book." Until then, I had no idea she was writing a book, but I wasn't surprised. Instantly, I felt proud. My mom is built differently—resilient, driven, and infused with an unshakable can-do attitude, all of which have been tested in unimaginable ways. She's also profoundly compassionate—a servant, confidant, and friend to grieving parents across the world. The moment I saw her message, I knew what the book was about and who it was for.

I still remember waking up earlier than usual on February 17, 2010. My wife and I had recently moved across the country, and I was settling into a new job. That morning, I made coffee, turned on the TV, and hopped on the stationary bike, utterly unaware that my life had already changed in ways I couldn't comprehend. My sister's life had changed. My mother's life had changed. Everything had changed—because my brother's life had ended.

Until that morning, I couldn't have imagined what it would feel like to lose my brother. All these years later, it's still impossible to put the deep sadness and ever-present sense of loss into words. For my mom, that sadness is even more profound, that sense of loss even more piercing. This book is her story—a journal of her journey from the darkest day of her life to the present. It's raw, honest, and reflective, documenting how she has navigated the unthinkable. It also reveals how her grief has fueled her passion to support others on their grief journey, creating supportive communities for parents whose lives were forever altered in a single moment.

This isn't a book of simple solutions or step-by-step instructions—because there are none. My mom doesn't offer checklists or timelines. Instead, she provides a lifeline. She shows grieving parents that they are not alone, that there is no "right" way to navigate grief, and that the unrelenting despair they experience is not a sign of failure—it's just part of the journey.

While every grieving parent's story is unique, the heartbreak, isolation, disorientation, and reinvention that follow the loss of a child are universal. If you're reading this, it's because you're searching for something: understanding, affirmation, or simply the knowledge that someone else gets it. Know that my mom does. She has been where you are, and she's here to walk beside you. Why Me? is a guide, a companion, and a source of light for anyone who feels lost in their grief. If you're seeking connection, community, or even a faint glimmer of a way forward, you've found a great place to begin.

To say I'm proud of my mom would be an understatement. She could have given in to despair and withdrawn from life. Instead, she chose to serve others, channeling her pain into a community, love, and healing mission. This book is yet another artifact of the beautiful legacy she continues to build in service of others and in my brother's memory.

Jeremiah

INTRODUCTION

One of the happiest days of my life was the day I gave birth to my beautiful son. From the moment he took his first breath, a son was born into a world of boundless potential. His tiny, perfect form filled my heart with overwhelming love, and I knew, at that moment, that my life had changed forever. His life began with the soft lullaby of hope and dreams, his tiny fingers clutching the hands of those who loved him.

As he grew, so did his curiosity and vitality, his every step a testament to the joy of life's unfolding journey. He ran through fields of laughter, his days filled with the warmth of friendship and the love of family, each moment adding color to the canvas of his existence. Every laugh, every milestone, filled me with pride. But nothing could have prepared me for the most sorrowful, despairing day of my life—the day he was tragically killed.

But as time marches on, even the brightest flames flicker. He entered adulthood with ambition and dreams, his heart overflowed with promises of a future yet to be written. He faced the world with unwavering determination, though life, as it often does, threw shadows in his path. And then, one day, the inevitable tragedy struck—sudden, cruel, and unrelenting.

The world that once seemed so full of promise now lay shattered. A life once filled with hope was snuffed out too soon, leaving only the aching void of loss. The sorrow of his passing clung to the hearts of those who knew him, their spirits heavy with the weight of what was lost—endless dreams never realized, laughter never heard again. In the wake of his absence, despair settled in, and the world seemed darker and colder. His departure left not just a gap in the lives of those who loved him but an emptiness that time could never fully heal.

At 27, my son was taken from me in a horrific accident, and with his passing, a part of my soul was torn away. The grief, the shock, the disbelief—I was crushed into a million broken pieces. The joy he had brought into my world was gone, leaving a void so deep it felt as if the very foundation of my life had shattered. I was left to navigate a world without him that will never be the same again. The pain is constant, and the emptiness is overwhelming, a cruel reminder of how quickly life can change.

In this book, "Why Me." I will take you on a journey through the depths of my grief, sharing the raw and unspoken truths of what it's like to endure the most devastating loss a mother can face. I will open my heart to you, revealing how I've navigated life with a broken heart, learning to survive in a world forever changed by my son's absence. This is not just a story of loss but of resilience, as I've fought each day to carry on despite the pain. It is a testament to the strength we never knew we had, even when everything feels shattered beyond repair.

Grief has a way of reshaping how we think and perceive the world around us. When we're in the throes of heart-wrenching loss, it's natural to ask, *"Why me?"*, *"How could this happen?"* or *"What did I do to deserve this?"* These questions often become unbidden, driven by the overwhelming pain that consumes us.

Loss also varies in its impact on different relationships. For instance, the grief of losing a sibling can, in some ways, rival the grief of a parent losing a child. Siblings not only mourn their brother or sister but also witness the profound, life-altering changes in their parents. This dual burden—grieving their sibling while also coping with the emotional absence of their parents—can feel overwhelming. Depending on the circumstances, siblings may suffer in ways that are uniquely their own.

As humans, we often believe that tragedies happen to others, not to us. This belief helps us navigate daily life without being paralyzed by fear. After all, how could anyone live fully while constantly worrying about losing their child? Telling ourselves, *"It won't happen to me,"* offers comfort—until the unimaginable does occur. And when it does, those haunting questions inevitably resurface: *"Why me?"*

This book, "*Why Me*," is meant to offer insight and guidance as you navigate the harrowing journey of grief. It explores the many challenges you may face along the way while reassuring you that your emotions, no matter how overwhelming, are valid and normal.

Through these pages, I hope to provide a sense of hope and peace. From my own experiences, I know that life can move forward and joy can eventually return, even after profound loss. My heartfelt wish is that "*Why Me*" offers you comfort, understanding, and the knowledge that you are not alone.

I hope to help you feel seen and understood by sharing my grief journey. While no two experiences of grief are exactly alike, the sorrow we feel is a universal thread that connects us all. I hope this book will help you navigate your grief and, in time, see that grief can evolve into something we learn to live with—like a quiet companion. It doesn't leave us but gently walks beside us, guiding us down memory lane with tenderness and love.

Chapter 1
The Stages of Grief - Need Not Apply

I have compiled the writings in this book from notes in my journal and some posts that I would write in my Facebook group, as well as my random thoughts and emotions. Some things I will say more than once in different chapters. It's because, through my journey, I have found it to be important.

If you are reading this book, most likely you have lost a child, or you may still be smothering in grief after years and searching for assistance to move forward and actively live again. In this book, "Why Me," I will share my gut-wrenching beginning and take you through some of my first fifteen years.

After child loss, you may find yourself surrounded by people who have all the answers, and they don't mind sharing them with you. Many of us are misled early on in our grief because of unwanted advice from those who have no idea what we are experiencing. We find ourselves not knowing what to do with all the emotions that have surfaced or how to deal with the excruciating pain that accompanies child loss.

Family and friends most likely will be talking behind your back, wishing you would just let it go and move on. They want the old you back. The general public doesn't allow us to grieve for any extended time. Many parents report having to return back to work within one week after facing the tragedy of losing their child or losing their job. There is currently legislation to change this to three months through the Leave Act. As of today (January 2025), a comprehensive "Leave Act" providing nationwide paid family leave has not passed in the United States; however, the existing "Family and Medical Leave Act

Why Me? - Navigating the Unbearable Truth of Grief and Loss

(FMLA)" allows for unpaid, job-protected leave for certain family and medical reasons, which was passed in 1993 with bipartisan support.

Our hell begins the moment we learn our child is gone. No matter the circumstances of their death, the result is the same: our child is no longer here, and our world is plunged into darkness. In the first days, weeks, or even months, our actions blur into a fog, and much of that time may feel like a blank slate we can barely recall.

We beg for our child back and do much bargaining; some often pretend their child is on vacation so as not to think about the death. Pretending doesn't change anything. Nothing works. Once the funeral is over and the world keeps spinning, we are often left alone to face our worst nightmare. This is when we come to know the true meaning of despair. We wander aimlessly, consumed by disbelief, searching for anything to numb the unbearable pain. We cry to God, "Why me? What did I do to deserve this?" We feel we're being punished. No amount of begging, promising, or bargaining helps, leaving us defeated.

Grief shatters us from the inside, leaving us struggling to breathe. As it tightens its grip, disbelief, panic, and an overwhelming sadness drowns us, creating a cocoon of darkness. Some days, anger surges like a wave, making us want to punch a wall. On other days, tears consume us entirely. In desperation, many parents turn to the internet, looking for anything to guide them through the pain. They come across the "five stages of grief" and feel as if they've found a lifeline—a formula for healing. If only it were that simple.

The Misunderstood Five Stages - There Are NO Stages of Grief

The five stages of grief—Denial, Anger, Bargaining, Depression, and Acceptance (DABDA)—were introduced in Elisabeth Kübler-Ross's

1969 book *On Death and Dying*. However, these stages were intended to describe the experiences of the *dying*, not those left behind to grieve. Kübler-Ross's groundbreaking work brought attention to the emotional needs of terminally ill patients, challenging the taboo of discussing death openly.

While her work revolutionized the care of the dying, the general public misinterpreted her stages as a universal roadmap for grief. Over time, this misunderstanding took root, leading many to believe that grieving follows a neat and orderly progression. But this couldn't be further from the truth.

For parents who have lost a child, the five stages do not apply. Grief is not linear. It is not a checklist or a series of steps to complete. Instead, it is a chaotic, unpredictable journey—a roller coaster of emotions or crashing waves that knock us down just when we think we're beginning to recover. Don't get me wrong, all these emotions will be experienced on your grief journey, but they will not be in any order, and some of them will happen over and over, while some may only happen once or twice. We never know until they happen.

The Reality of Grief

Grief is deeply personal and unique. While many of us experience similar emotions, they do not follow a set sequence or timeline. There is no "right" way to grieve, yet society's fixation on the five stages can leave us feeling as though we're failing at grief. Parents often express frustration, confusion, and despair when they don't reach "acceptance" quickly or when their emotions seem to cycle endlessly. For me, I'm not clear on acceptance. I know that my son is no longer here. I know he is dead, but acceptance is a tough one for me. Can a parent ever accept it fully? I don't know.

Some people experience complicated grief—a state where the loss consumes them completely. Life feels meaningless, joy seems impossible, and even the simplest routines become a struggle. Isolation sets in, accompanied by deep sadness, endless "what ifs" and "should haves," and, at times, thoughts of giving up entirely. I know

Why Me? - Navigating the Unbearable Truth of Grief and Loss

this all too well because I was in that place for quite a while. But I made it through.

Debilitating grief doesn't improve with time. A person may not allow themselves to feel, which keeps them in a crippling state of grief and not accepting that their life will be different now and not trying to adjust to it.

Denial, for instance, is often misunderstood. It isn't harmful in moderation—it's a natural defense mechanism. After losing a child, our brains protect us by processing the truth in manageable doses. Over time, we must face the reality of our loss, but rushing this process can be detrimental.

Grief requires us to engage with our emotions as they arise. There is no avoiding it. Attempting to suppress or outrun grief only intensifies its hold on us. The only way through is to confront each wave as it comes, no matter how overwhelming.

Breaking Free from the "Stages"

Grief is not a race or a challenge. It's a deeply human experience that defies structure. Clinging to the concept of stages can limit our healing and create unnecessary guilt or shame. Grief is not a list—it is a series of raw, unfiltered emotions that ebb and flow.

Triggers, such as a song, a scent, or the sight of another child, can send us spiraling back into deep grief, no matter how much time has passed. This is normal. Grief doesn't have a finish line, and healing is not about "moving on" but about learning to carry the pain and live alongside it.

Kübler-Ross herself acknowledged that grief does not follow a predictable path. Toward the end of her career, she regretted how her stages had been misunderstood. So let go of the stages and focus instead on the natural flow of your emotions.

We are members of a club no one wants to join, our dues paid in the most unimaginable way. Child loss does not come with a manual or a map—only grief. But in time, you may discover a strength within yourself that you never knew existed.

Shirley Tripp Johnson

Allow yourself to feel. Allow yourself to heal. Your grief will guide you when the time is right. Grief is not something to conquer but something to experience, day by day, moment by moment. Remember: there are no stages, only your unique journey through an emotion that changes us forever.

As you navigate your grief journey, no matter how unbearable it feels, hold on to hope. Shifting your focus to what you still have can make a difference. At times, it may not seem like it, but thinking about your family or someone or something that means the world to you can help keep you afloat. When it feels like you're gasping for air, struggling in waters that threaten to pull you under, keep treading—you are stronger than you think.

You have to feel to heal.

Chapter 2
Tragedy Strikes

In November 2009, Tripp moved to Pennsylvania from Arkansas, where he had lived for many years after moving from Michigan to attend the University of Arkansas. I was glad to have him back with us after so many years of living in Arkansas and only getting to visit a couple of times a year. He planned to go back to Arkansas in March 2010 to get his truck and more of his belongings. His sister, Deidre, had a Honda Civic that he was driving until he could get his truck up to Pennsylvania.

At the time, I had been laid off from work and was designing websites from home. A Construction remodeler called MC Contractors hired me to design a website for his company, and a few days after Tripp had been in Pennsylvania, Mike, the owner of the company, stopped by to pay me for some work I had completed on his website. Mike was a tall, friendly Black man with a warm demeanor that made people feel instantly at ease. He walked in, made himself comfortable, and enthusiastically complimented me on my improvements to his site. His easygoing nature and genuine appreciation for my work made him a pleasure to be around.

When I introduced him to Tripp, I mentioned that Tripp was looking for a job. Mike immediately took a liking to him. Without hesitation, he turned to Tripp and asked, "What all can you do, Tripp?" and Tripp replied, "I can do just about anything. "Mike said, "I'll pick you up at 6 a.m. tomorrow and give you a try."

Mike's kindness and willingness to help a stranger left a lasting impression. His generosity set the stage for what would become a meaningful connection with both Tripp and myself. and his support came at a time when Tripp needed it most.

That night, Tripp and I stayed up talking about Mike and the opportunity he had offered. While Tripp was a little hesitant about going to work for someone he had just met, he couldn't hide his excitement. We talked until midnight, going over what the day might bring and imagining what it would be like.

The next morning, Tripp eagerly waited for Mike's arrival; his anticipation showed. As soon as Mike pulled up, Tripp was ready to dive in. He started working for Mike and quickly became a favorite among everyone on the job. With his dazzling smile, respectful demeanor, and boundless energy, Tripp had a natural ability to brighten any room he walked into. He carried himself with pride, head held high and chest out as if to announce, "I'm here."

Many nights, Tripp would return home late, not because the work dragged on but because Mike had taken him out for a massage or invited him to hang out for a few hours after work. In what felt like no time at all, their professional relationship evolved into a genuine friendship. Mike became not just a boss but also a mentor and a friend, someone Tripp could laugh with, learn from, and lean on during this new chapter of his life.

Tripp was 27, a grown man, but to me, he was still my baby, and I cherished the little routines we shared. Every morning, I'd get up early to fix him a good lunch before he left for work. I'd listen for the familiar sound of him bouncing down the stairs, his energy filling the house. His face always lit up with a big smile as he greeted me with his cheerful, "Good morning, Mama!"

His cologne was always so strong. He wore Usher, and if we were in the car together, I would begin to gag and would have to roll the window down to breathe. He loved his cologne.

I'd hand him his lunch, and just like clockwork, I'd get my hug and hear him say, "I love you, Mama," before he headed out the door. "I'll call ya later!" he'd call back over his shoulder as he climbed into his car. Standing at the window, I'd wave him off, watching until his car disappeared down the road.

Some nights, though, long after I had gone to bed, I'd wake up and find Tripp downstairs. At 3 a.m., he'd often be sitting at the dining room table, what I lovingly referred to as *romancing a bowl of cereal,* with the lights dimmed low. There was something almost poetic about the way he enjoyed those quiet moments. I never said a word because I knew he didn't like to be disturbed when he was eating his cereal—it was his time.

Those small rituals, both morning and night, became such a special part of my life with Tripp. They were moments of connection, comfort, and love that I hold close to my heart even now.

I loved that boy so very much. Our daily rituals were simple but full of love. True to his word, Tripp would always call me during his lunch break. He'd share little stories about his day, whether it was how work was going or something funny that had happened. Those calls meant the world to me, just like the mornings we shared. It's those small, everyday moments that I treasure the most, reminders of the deep bond we had.

In February 2010, we had a huge snowfall that kept Tripp off work due to the extremely bad road conditions. Despite having lived in Michigan for several years, where snow was a common occurrence, he was still amazed by how much snow piled up over those few hours.

Tripp took it upon himself to go outside every hour to use the snowblower, determined to keep up with the constant snowfall. He wasn't just clearing our driveway; he also helped our neighbors, especially the elderly couple across the street who had a harder time dealing with the snow. He seemed to genuinely enjoy going out to help, never complaining about the cold or the effort.

In between snow-blowing sessions, Tripp would come inside, lay down, and catch a quick nap for an hour before heading back out again. It was a constant cycle, but he did it with a smile and a sense of purpose. It was just the way he was—always thinking of others and lending a hand without being asked.

Tripp's sister, Deidre, lived nearby in Blandon, about twenty-five minutes away, and they were very close. He spent a lot of time with her, as family meant everything to him. He often commented that he wished his Bubba didn't live so far away. Jeremiah and his wife Sarah

Why Me? - Navigating the Unbearable Truth of Grief and Loss

lived in Boise, Idaho. Tripp, since a little boy, had always called his older brother Bubba. In addition to his close-knit family, Tripp also began building a circle of new friends. One of his favorite pastimes became playing poker at a bar and restaurant called Tailgaters Steakhouse.

On the evening of February 16th, 2009, Tripp decided to head out to Tailgaters for a few rounds of poker before returning to work the next day. He stayed out later than usual, enjoying the game, and didn't get home until quite late.

On the morning of February 17, 2010, at 6:00 a.m., I got up and made Tripp's lunch as he came bouncing down the stairs, eager to get back to work after a few days off due to the snow. "Good morning, Mama!" he called out cheerfully. As usual, I stood there with his lunch pail in hand, savoring the simple routine.

I will never forget our last moments together. Tripp opened the door, and the cold air rushed in, the ground still covered with snow. Standing tall, he puffed out his chest and said with a smile, "It's a beautiful day, Mama." After giving me his usual big hug, he headed out the door, calling back, "I love you, Mama; I'll call you later," as he climbed into the car. I waved until he was out of sight, never imagining that would be the last time I'd see his beautiful smile, feel his tight hugs, or hear his sweet, laughter-filled voice.

I always had the morning news on before I started working, but that morning, for some reason, I didn't. Looking back now, I believe it was God protecting me because if I had seen the news, I would have jumped in my car and rushed to the scene. I probably would have ended up in handcuffs because I would have been fighting whoever got in my way trying to get to my boy. Instead, I went straight to my office to begin designing a website for a cross-fit company in Ohio. By the time it was around 10 a.m., I decided to head upstairs to shower and get ready for lunch with some former coworkers.

As I was drying my hair after the shower, I heard Perry, our poodle, barking. I turned off the hairdryer and glanced out the bedroom

Shirley Tripp Johnson

window. To my shock, I saw two state trooper cars parked in front of our house. My heart sank as I wondered what was happening.

"Hmmm, I wonder what this is all about," I thought, assuming something was happening in the neighborhood. I went downstairs and opened the door. The two troopers stood there, their expressions serious as they asked if I was Shirley Johnson, and I told them yes. They asked to come inside. Confused and in a bit of a rush, as it was already 10:45, I let them in.

"What's going on?" I asked.

"Does Tripp Taylor live here?" they asked.

Still unaware, I laughed and said, "Well, it depends. What did he do?" But their faces didn't change—solemn and unyielding. I had no idea that my world was about to shatter.

"Ma'am, we need you to sit down," one of them said firmly.

Confused, I asked, "Why? Just tell me. What's going on? Did something happen?"

"We need you to sit down," they repeated.

I couldn't understand why sitting down was so important. All I wanted was a quick explanation so I could finish drying my hair and make it to lunch with my friends.

I could tell that no matter what, they weren't going to say anything unless I sat down. I led them to the living room, sat on the couch, and looked up as they stood before me, their posture straight and their tone grave.

Looking up at the two troopers, I began to feel a rising sense of worry. "What is it?" I asked, my voice shaking. "What is it?"

"Ma'am, your son was in an accident this morning," one of them said gently.

"Where? Is he okay?" I asked, the panic rising in my chest.

"Ma'am, your son Tripp has been in an accident in front of the Perkiomen School on Route 73."

Why Me? - Navigating the Unbearable Truth of Grief and Loss

I squinted and frowned, shaking my head. "That's impossible," I said. "It's almost 11 a.m., and Tripp left the house at 6:15 am this morning."

"It's not him," I insisted.

The officer's expression softened as he gently replied, "Ma'am, the accident happened around 7:30 a.m. this morning."

My voice wavered as I asked, "Is he hurt? How badly is he hurt?"

The officer looked down; his head bowed. When he raised his eyes, his words shattered my world.

"Your son died at the scene," he said quietly.

"He didn't survive, ma'am," the trooper said solemnly.

"No, that can't be true!" I cried. "He left for work hours ago. It can't be him. He's with his boss, driving to Philadelphia for a job."

"No, ma'am," the officer said softly. "They were in a silver Honda Civic, and his boss was driving. They were hit by a school bus this morning."

I screamed, "Nooooooo, not Tripp! This can't happen to him, to our family!" The anguish tore through me as I fell to my knees, sobbing uncontrollably. I began hitting the knees of the two officers, screaming, "What a horrible thing to come and tell me! It can't be true! It can't be true!" Tears streamed down my face, pouring like a river, as I tried to comprehend the incomprehensible.

"Get out of my house!" I screamed. "Get out!"

"Ma'am, we cannot leave you alone until someone gets here," one of the officers said, their voices calm but firm.

"I don't want you here! Just leave!" I shouted, but they stood their ground, unmoving, their faces filled with compassion and sorrow.

From A news article: Poust, delivering students to the middle school that morning, turned left to enter the school driveway without first stopping on the roadway

and collided with the oncoming car that Carroll was driving.

Reviewing tapes from the bus's video system, investigators said the videos also showed Poust failing to come to a complete stop at 10 different stop signs before the accident.

In addition, authorities said the videos showed Poust displaying signs of fatigue, inattentiveness, and carelessness throughout the trip that morning. The videos captured Poust, who had a second job at night and had not slept for at least 24 hours before the accident, rubbing his eyes and face numerous times in the hour just before the crash, the criminal complaint said.

Poust had a second job working security from 10 p.m. to 6 a.m. at Souderton Mennonite Home. His last full

Why Me? - Navigating the Unbearable Truth of Grief and Loss

sleep was on the night of Feb. 15 into the morning of Feb. 16, according to authorities.

Trying to gather myself, I got up and tried to think of what to do next, but my mind was spinning. The first thing I did was call one of the women I was supposed to have lunch with. Through sobs, I told her, "I'm not going to make it. My son... my son was just killed in an accident." I still wonder even now why I thought to call Cindy first,

The next call was to my daughter, Deidre, then to my son, Jeremiah, and finally to my husband, Dan. I will never forget the heavy silence on the other end of the line when I made those telephone calls as they struggled to process the news I had just shared. Time seemed to freeze. I paced the room, asking the officers questions, desperate for answers, but they could only tell me that I would need to speak with the detective on the case. They handed me a few phone numbers and began guiding me through what the process would entail.

When Dan and Deidre arrived, they threw their arms around me, their faces wet with tears. We held each other tightly, crying and trembling. A piece of our family was gone, ripped from us in an instant. The devastation was unbearable.

When I heard about Tripp being killed, the shock left me feeling numb—almost as if a shield had formed around me, protecting me from the full weight of the pain. The numbness kept the brokenness at bay, or at least, it kept it from consuming me all at once. The next few days are pretty blurry to me. The numbness and fog had only gotten worse, and I felt like I wasn't even in existence. I moved through those hours and days in a haze, unable to comprehend the reality of what had happened. It felt as if time had lost all meaning, and I was floating in a void, detached from everything around me. The world continued to turn, but mine had stopped. I kept trying to wake up, hoping it was a bad dream.

My children, Deidre and Jeremiah, both agreed with me that cremating Tripp was the best choice. However, his dad's family strongly disagreed. They wanted him buried in a family plot they owned in Russellville, Arkansas. After a heated argument, we ultimately agreed to fly his body to Arkansas and lay him to rest there. I wasn't happy with the decision, but to avoid more conflict and bickering, I accepted it.

The next couple of days that followed were a whirlwind. It felt as though a protective veil surrounded me as I made phone calls—making arrangements, notifying loved ones, booking flights, and receiving countless calls from people everywhere; I was utterly numb and exhausted. It was as if I were in a bubble, shielded somehow, allowing me to think clearly—at least on the surface. Deep down, I couldn't truly believe my son was gone. I kept clinging to the hope that this was all just a terrible dream, desperate to wake up and escape this nightmare.

Tripp had touched so many hearts and had friends scattered far and wide. The outpouring of love and support was overwhelming, a testament to the impact he had on so many lives.

The next day my husband, Dan, and I drove down to the coroner's office in Norristown, Pennsylvania, to pick up Tripp's belongings. When we arrived, we were led to a small, gray room with a steel table and a few chairs. The room had no color at all—it felt cold and lifeless, like death itself.

After a short wait, a woman came in and sat down—I think she was the coroner's assistant—I was sobbing and asking questions about Tripp. I was so worried about him being stuck in a vault so alone. She tried to assure me he was ok and they would take care of him. She handed me a brown paper bag. I still have that bag. Inside were a wallet, a cell phone, a pair of sunglasses, a belt, some loose change, a few bucks, and some candy wrappers. That was it. No clothes, nothing else. Just a small bag of ordinary items. It was devastating to think that this was all I had left. A damn brown paper bag.

I asked her where Tripp's clothes were, and she explained that they had to be cut off of him and were destroyed, including the work boots he'd been wearing. The thought made me feel like I was going to vomit. Cut off? Why? She didn't have an answer and directed me

Why Me? - Navigating the Unbearable Truth of Grief and Loss

back to the detective. I didn't pursue it further—I couldn't bear to know more at that point. I was already sick just thinking about it all.

I asked to see Tripp, desperate to lay eyes on him and make sure he was okay. But I was told it wasn't allowed. "You wouldn't want to leave," the assistant said gently.

"I promise I will leave," I pleaded. "I just need to see my baby and make sure he's okay."

She tried to reassure me. "I assure you, Mrs. Johnson, we are taking very good care of him until he's transported to the funeral home. I promise."

I begged, but it didn't matter. She wouldn't relent. I guess I understood on some level, but my heart didn't. It felt like I was being torn apart, unable to see my boy one last time.

I remember going to shop for a new dress for Tripp's funeral, sobbing the entire time. When I walked into the store, my mind was a blur. I was wandering, not knowing what I was doing, when an African American woman approached me. She was a heavy-set woman with flawless makeup and a warm, compassionate presence, though a few of her teeth were missing. Despite that, her smile was genuine and full of care. She looked at me with concern and asked if I was okay.

I told her no, I was not ok, and that I was looking for a dress for a funeral. Without hesitation, she pulled me into a tight, comforting hug. In that moment, it felt like the Lord Himself was holding me. Her embrace was so strong, so full of love and understanding; it gave me a sense of peace I hadn't known in days. It was as if, for just a moment, the weight of my grief was shared, and I wasn't carrying it alone.

She asked if I was a believer, and I told her yes. Then, with a gentle voice, she asked, "Was it your son who was killed in that horrific crash on Wednesday morning?" How did she know? Still holding me close, I nodded, unable to speak.

Shirley Tripp Johnson

She released me and asked me to tell her about Tripp. I shared how he had just moved back with us after living in Arkansas and had only been with us for three short months before this tragedy. She smiled at me, and as I looked into her face, her smile was that of an Angel. I thought she was beautiful, and I felt an incredible sense of connection with her.

She began to speak softly. "Honey, the good Lord knew what He was doing. He sent him home to be with you before his return to glory with the Lord." I will never forget those words. She was so comforting, loving, and compassionate. She helped me find the perfect outfit for the funeral, and I will forever remember her name—Emma. I will never forget her kindness and the way she showed me God's love when I needed it most.

We arrived in Russellville, Arkansas, on a Saturday, February 20th, 2010, and I immediately went to Humphrey Funeral Home. I had grown up with the funeral director, Jim Bob, so I didn't hesitate to demand answers. "Where's Tripp?" I asked as soon as I saw him.

Jim Bob told me they had just returned with his body, but he hadn't been uncrated yet. "I want to see him right now!" I insisted.

"Not until we get him ready," Jim Bob replied.

Knowing Jim as I did—and fueled by my determination as a mother—I refused to back down. "I will go through every room in this building if you don't take me to him right now. And I mean it."

Reluctantly, Jim Bob agreed and led me to a room where a box rested on a table, almost like a gurney. "Give me a hammer," I demanded. "I'll get him out of the box myself."

Jim Bob hesitated but handed me a claw hammer. I started to pry the box open, but I was having some trouble as I was shaking so badly. I handed the claw hammer back to Jim Bob and he opened the box. and there he was—my sweet baby boy. He was wrapped in clear plastic, lying there so still, eyes closed like he was sleeping. I asked to be left alone, and as Jim Bob turned to leave, he asked if I would be okay.

Why Me? - Navigating the Unbearable Truth of Grief and Loss

"I'm not okay," I said flatly. "My baby is dead. I just need to be alone with him."

It was the first time I had seen him since he walked out the door on that awful day—the day my life felt like it ended, too. His body was stiff since he had already been embalmed in Pennsylvania before they could fly him back to Arkansas.

He was beautiful. My boy, lying there with his eyes closed, looking so peaceful. But I felt anything but peaceful. I was shattered. I began to cry, talking to him, begging him to let this all be a terrible dream. "Please," I prayed, "let me wake up. Please, Tripp, come back to me." I begged, I prayed, I screamed, and I cursed, but nothing brought him back.

Slowly, I started unwrapping him, unsure of what injuries I might find beneath the plastic. I didn't know how I'd react if I saw something I couldn't handle, but I had to keep going. There was a black spot on his thumb and his wrist where it had been punctured, but that was all. Relief washed over me—he was perfect aside from that.

I don't know how long I stayed in that room. Time felt frozen as I rubbed his head, ran my fingers through his hair, and held his hand, sobbing uncontrollably. Eventually, I heard someone come in—it was Tripp's cousin, JR, who also worked at the funeral home.

"Come on, Shirley," he said gently. "We need to do some work on Tripp, but you can come back tomorrow."

I looked at JR and said firmly, "I'll be back tomorrow to do his hair and makeup myself. I don't want you all to do it. I brought the clothes I want him buried in. Get him dressed, and I'll handle the rest."

He nodded in agreement. I bent over, kissed my boy, and left. Walking out of that room felt surreal like I was in a dream. Nothing felt real. I was numb, trapped in disbelief.

Tripp used to joke that if anything ever happened to him, we should just send him down the river in a wooden pine box. And in a way, that's exactly what we did. While we didn't float him down the river,

Shirley Tripp Johnson

we chose a beautiful pine casket, trimmed with gold and lined with a gorgeous cream-colored silk pall.

I returned to the funeral home the next day. Tripp was dressed in jeans, a Pink Floyd T-shirt, and his favorite button-up shirt worn slightly open. He looked just like himself, and it brought me a strange sense of comfort.

As I approached him, I started talking to him—not with tears this time, but with the gentle love of a mama speaking to her boy. I told him how much I loved him and how deeply I was going to miss him.

His hair was slightly messy, so I gently brushed it, admiring the thick, gorgeous locks that I knew so well. Taking my time, I carefully applied a little makeup to his handsome face, ensuring every detail was just right. "Perfect," I murmured. "You look perfect, Tripp."

The funeral home had provided some lip colors, but they didn't feel right—they weren't *his*. Reaching into my purse, I pulled out my lipstick and gently dabbed it onto his lips. It was a soft pink—subtle, just enough to add a little color that suited him perfectly.

I stepped back, studying him with a bittersweet smile. "Perfect," I whispered again. "You look perfect, buddy." But then I paused—something was missing. "Wait," I said softly. "Your sunglasses need to go on top of your head, just like you always wore them."

I smoothed his hair once more, making sure everything was just right, and carefully placed the sunglasses on his head. Stepping back again, I took a deep breath and smiled through the ache. "There," I whispered. "Perfect."

I'm not going to include all the turmoil that arose during that time. We were supposed to stay at Tripp's dad's house—the same house where Tripp had lived with his father before moving to Pennsylvania. Unfortunately, that didn't work out very well. There were some tense and unfriendly conversations with that side of the family the second day we were there, so we ended up leaving and getting a hotel room, where we stayed for the remainder of the trip. All I'll say is this: it was quite unpleasant when someone—not Tripp's mom or dad—tried to take control of everything. That didn't sit well with me at all.

Some of Tripp's best friends, Kyle, Brandt, Dustin, and Jim, traveled from Michigan and Nick from California to be here, and when they arrived, they gathered at a bar-restaurant, meeting up unexpectedly with some of Tripp's local friends there. It was such a special moment to see everyone come together like that. His friends were incredible—each one of them brought so much love and support. It had been a while since I had seen those boys, so it was really good to see them again, but I wish it hadn't been under these circumstances.

The visitation was the evening before we laid Tripp to rest on February 22, 2010. The outpouring of love was incredible—hundreds of people came to pay their respects. I saw people I hadn't seen in years and met so many of the kid's friends that I didn't know. I was amazed at so much support for all of us from so many.

We held the funeral at the Pottsville Baptist. At the funeral the next day, there were so many attendees that not everyone could fit inside the church. It was standing room only, with people even gathered outside. It was clear how deeply Tripp was loved by so many.

On the way to the gravesite, his father, Rick, and one of his friends led the hearse on their Harley-Davidson motorcycles, ensuring that every car pulled to the side of the road in respect. Too often, people don't show reverence for a hearse carrying a loved one, but Rick made sure that Tripp was honored that day. It was a fitting tribute to a life that had touched so many.

Shirley Tripp Johnson

I've never seen so many people gather at the gravesite after the funeral. It was a testament to how much Tripp meant to everyone. His gravesite was beautiful, nestled beneath a tree with a peaceful creek behind it—a perfect resting place for him. Everyone who knew Tripp Taylor understood the magic of his presence—he had a way of lighting up any room and ensuring everyone had a great time. Charming and funny, honest and sincere, Tripp was the kind of person whose infectious laugh and big, goofy grin could brighten even the darkest day. He was impossible to stay mad at and so easy to love, earning a special place in the hearts of everyone fortunate enough to know him. Now, my baby was gone, and I was left with a hollow shell.

The drive to the airport to go back home was quiet and heavy with sorrow. I couldn't shake the feeling that something wasn't right about leaving Tripp behind, but deep down, I knew he wasn't there in that grave. His soul had risen to be with the Lord, and that thought comforted me.

Why Me? - Navigating the Unbearable Truth of Grief and Loss

2 Corinthians 5:8-To be absent from the body is to be present with the Lord.

I was still numb, caught in a fog. It all felt like a bad dream, and all I wanted was to wake up from it. One thing that brought me comfort was finding a letter that Tripp wrote to Dan and me after he was stopped one night and ended up in Jail for a DUI. The end of this letter touched me so. Tripp gave his life to the Lord on my birthday, 12/22/91, and in this letter, he is remembering that day. Here is what it says.

> "I want God in my life again. I still can remember to this day at Fellowship of Christians, where I stood up and made confessions. That was the best feeling in my life, and I believe it was the 22 of December (My Mommy's B-Day). Well, I just wanted to write you guys a letter. And I really appreciate everything you guys have ever done for me. I LOVE YOU BOTH MORE Thank I SHOW IT. I Love Both & Always, Tripp

I'll never forget the day it all began for him. I watched as he trembled in church, visibly moved. He turned to me and asked, "What do I do?" Leaning in, I whispered, "The Lord is speaking to you." Without hesitation, he said, "I'm going to the front." I smiled as he walked forward, publicly professing his faith in Christ and accepting the Lord as his Savior. It was a moment etched in my heart forever.

Shirley Tripp Johnson

Chapter 3

My Broken Heart is Never Going to Heal

As I sat there, hollow and broken, I felt like I was drowning in despair. Some days, I wasn't sure I could go on. One night, my husband asked me, "What's the difference between losing Tripp and losing your parents and all your siblings?" I paused, uncertain whether to answer. Before I could respond, I made him promise not to call 911 twice. When he finally gave me his word, I admitted the truth: suicide. The pain of losing Tripp was so unbearable I didn't want to live. I couldn't see a way forward.

In the beginning, I just wanted to die. The pain was so overwhelming that I couldn't imagine continuing to live with it. Each day felt like a question mark—I didn't know if I could keep going. I was in uncharted territory, struggling to stay afloat, and it felt like I was drowning. I was so exhausted, and my heart ached so deeply that I was certain it would simply stop beating.

Losing my son shattered me in ways I never thought possible. The grief was relentless, suffocating, and all-encompassing. I cried almost constantly, sometimes for hours on end, unable to stop the flood of emotions. Even sleep, when it came, offered no relief. I would wake up in the middle of the night, sobbing uncontrollably, as though my heart was breaking all over again in my dreams.

The loss invaded every corner of my life. Intimacy with my husband vanished; I couldn't bring myself to be vulnerable in that way. I felt like Tripp could see me, and the thought filled me with guilt and

Why Me? - Navigating the Unbearable Truth of Grief and Loss

shame. It was as if the bond between mother and child, even in death, cast a shadow over my marriage.

I was broken—shattered into a million tiny pieces with no idea how to put myself back together. Every day felt like I was trapped in an endless storm of sorrow, and I truly came to understand the meaning of despair. There was no light, no way out, just a relentless ache that I thought would never ease.

I found myself watching the video from Tripp's funeral over and over, just to see his face again. I had his pictures all around me, and I would stare at them until tears poured from my eyes like endless oceans. I didn't want to answer the phone, go anywhere, or see anyone. All I wanted was to die.

I didn't go out much, but whenever I had to drive somewhere, I often found myself wondering—if I sped up and hit something, would it just injure me badly or end everything? Then I'd shake my head to snap out of it and remind myself of Jeremiah and Deidre.

The only thing that kept me here was the thought of my other children, Deidre and Jeremiah, and my husband, Dan. I knew I couldn't leave them, but I felt like I was failing as a mother and a wife.

My mind was a whirlwind of chaos, a storm I couldn't calm. My heart felt as though a vital piece had been ripped away, leaving an emptiness so profound that even drawing breath seemed impossible without it. The pain was relentless, searing through every part of me—a pain unlike anything I had ever known. How could anyone endure something so all-consuming, so devastatingly unbearable? It was as if my entire being had been shattered, and the pieces refused to fit back together.

For the rest of 2010, not a single day passed where I didn't wish for the pain to end, even if it meant dying. I told myself Dan would be okay without me—but my children? I was their mom, and deep down, I realized I probably needed them more than they needed me. If I could have pulled them all inside my heart to help me carry the weight of my grief, I would have. But instead, I withdrew, wanting nothing more than to be left alone—isolated and broken.

Shirley Tripp Johnson

My grief was so overwhelming that I had nothing left to give. Every time Jeremiah or Deidre called, I would sob uncontrollably. I worried they might think I loved Tripp more than them, but that wasn't true. I loved them all equally. But now, my youngest was gone, and I didn't know how to process the loss. My heart ached for Jeremiah and Deidre. I tried so hard to hold it together, but I couldn't. I knew they were hurting too, and I wanted to be strong for them, but I was completely shattered. I couldn't manage my grief, let alone be the steady presence they needed after losing their brother.

It must have been so painful for them to hear and see their mom in such a broken state. The sobbing was uncontrollable, and I hated that they had to witness it. I loved them more than anything in this world, but our family was fractured in a way I didn't know how to heal.

One thing you quickly learn after a devastating loss is how much you need your friends. Living in Pennsylvania, the only close friend I had nearby was Joyce. She lived about an hour and a half away in Mount Joy, Pennsylvania, while my other two best friends were farther away—Gwen in Arkansas and Erica in Virginia.

Joyce was my rock after Tripp was killed. Every time I talked to her, I cried like a baby, and she was always there with love and compassion. Even though she'd never had children of her own, the way she comforted me was irreplaceable. Gwen was supportive, too, though I didn't talk to her as often.

Erica, on the other hand, surprised me. She was the one I thought would be the most supportive, but instead, she pulled away. She couldn't handle my grief. What? I couldn't handle my grief either—I wasn't asking her to fix it. I just needed her to be there. The hurt and anger I felt toward her ran deep. In my pain, I wrote her a message on Facebook. I wasn't kind; I shamed her and said some truly mean things. After that, she unfriended me, and we haven't spoken since.

It still breaks my heart to think that a friend could walk away during the darkest, most devastating time of my life. But through it all, I still had Joyce and Gwen—and they were enough.

Why Me? - Navigating the Unbearable Truth of Grief and Loss

There was no fixing it. No amount of praying or begging could bring Tripp back. The weight of that reality crushed me, and I felt helpless.

And my poor husband, Dan. What I put him through. He was my rock, my unwavering support, even when I was anything but easy to love. He stood by me through the darkest moments, loving me when I couldn't even love myself.

I remember how I'd change my pajamas right before he got home from work, so he wouldn't know I'd stayed in the same thing all day. In the beginning, there were times when I didn't take a shower for two weeks. I hated showers. I hated anything that required effort—anything that forced me to move. My days blurred together, going from the bed to the couch and back again.

Sometimes, I'd catch myself smiling or even laughing for a moment, only to suddenly break down in tears. I started calling those moments "Sappy and Had"—sorrowful one minute, managing a smile the next, or feeling a flicker of joy before collapsing into sobs. Joy was so hard to find. But over time, I realized joy could be anything that turned the corners of my lips up, even for just a fleeting moment.

I tried to embrace those moments, but the guilt of feeling happy when Tripp was gone weighed heavy on me. It didn't make sense—how could I let joy in when he wasn't here to share it? The battle between grief and the smallest glimmers of happiness was constant, and it left me feeling torn.

I would cry out to God, overwhelmed by the weight of it all: "Lord, I can't live with this pain—I just can't. How am I supposed to go on? I can't function, I can't breathe, I can't think. I'm shattered, and this pain is crushing me. Please, Lord, take it away. I can't live like this. I just can't."

When I was alone, I would break down completely. I'd hit the walls, collapse to the floor, and sob uncontrollably, lay in bed clutching Tripp's pillow. "How can this be happening?" I'd cry out. "Lord, please bring my baby back. I'll do anything—just please, bring him back to me. I can't do this. I can't. I just want this pain to end."

Shirley Tripp Johnson

The grief was so overwhelming I could hardly swallow. Dark thoughts crept in, and I found myself crying out, "Lord, I don't want to keep going like this. Please, I'm begging you—help me. Why did you let my son die? What did I do to deserve this?" In my anguish, I lashed out: "I hate this. I hate you." It was raw, unfiltered, and the deepest expression of my unbearable pain.

I knew deep down that I didn't hate God—I loved Him. But I was angry, and in my grief, I blamed Him for everything that had happened. I knew better, but at that moment, the anger was consuming, and the pain was unbearable. I was completely shattered, broken, and hurting in ways I never imagined possible.

About three months after Tripp was killed, I received a phone call from my nephew Earl. Earl is a pastor in the town of Russellville, where I grew up and where Tripp is buried. He officiated Tripp's funeral service. He called to check on me and asked how I was doing.

"I'm mad at God," I admitted. "He took Tripp away from me and our family."

Earl listened patiently as I sobbed and ranted about God taking Tripp and then asked, "When you were mad at Papa (my daddy), what did you do?"

"I told him," I said simply.

"Well, that's what you need to do with the Father," Earl said. "He understands, Shirley. If you just talk to Him, He will release you from that anger. Go pray."

After we hung up, I went up to Tripp's bedroom and fell to the floor, consumed by my emotions. I cried, screamed, and even cussed as I poured my heart out to God. "Why, God? Why did You let this happen? Bring Tripp back to me! If You won't bring him back, then please—please—take this anger away from me. I know this isn't Your fault; it's the fault of the driver of that damn bus. But I can't carry this anger anymore. Please, God, help me."

I don't know how long I lay face down on the floor, tears streaming, feeling utterly shattered. But eventually, as I opened my eyes and slowly began to lift myself up, something felt... different. It was as though a part of me had been washed clean. The crushing weight of my anger had lifted, leaving me with a sense of clarity and renewal. From that moment on, the anger I once held against God never returned.

I stood to my feet, raised my arms toward the heavens, and thanked God with every fiber of my being. "Thank You, Lord, for taking this anger at you from me. I love You. Thank You, thank You. Amen."

I was so angry with God and blamed Him for taking Tripp. How could this possibly be His plan? At first, I couldn't see past my rage. But over time, I realized that so many mothers who lose a child feel the same way—they blame God. I mean, who else is there to blame, right?

Wrong.

It's natural to be angry, and since God is the ruler of Heaven and Earth, we assume He should have stopped it from happening. But the truth is, it wasn't God who took my son. It was a man not paying attention. It seems when anything goes wrong, it's God's fault, but what about all the times we have been blessed, like with the birth of that child we are now grieving?

And yet, no matter the cause, the loss of a child is an indescribable tragedy. The pain is beyond words. People often say, "I can't even imagine what you're going through." And my response is always the same: "If you can't imagine it, I can't explain it."

Then some try to comfort you with advice or comparisons. "I know how you feel—I lost my sibling." Or, "I lost my parents," or even, "My dog died." Are you kidding me? You don't know *anything*. There is no greater pain than losing a child. They were a part of us, literally—they grew inside us for nine months, and their DNA remains within us forever.

And let's not forget the canned responses. "They're in a better place." Really? When you've lost a child, there is no better place for them than right here with you. Maybe in Heaven, we'll understand, and maybe then we'll find peace. But right now, in the middle of the heartbreak, that kind of statement doesn't help. Even if a child was suffering from a terrible disease and had no hope of recovery, no parent *wanted* their child to die.

The truth is, losing a child is a pain that defies explanation, and unless you've lived it, you'll never truly understand.

The year 2010 was unbearably heavy, and my grief echoed loudly in the silence of being alone. It stung at every turn, piercing through even the smallest moments. I stopped cooking for Dan, leaving him to come home after a long day and prepare meals himself. I simply couldn't function. It felt like I was losing my mind, consumed entirely by the pain.

Each day seemed worse than the last, and every morning I doubted I'd make it through. When Dan came home, I tried to mask my despair, though I think he knew. I'm sure he wondered if our lives would ever return to normal. But I didn't feel normal. I didn't even feel whole. I was hollow—just a shell of who I once was.

When school started back in September 2010, I was a wreck. School buses became a painful trigger for me. Every morning, when the bus stopped in front of our house to pick up the children, I had to turn my head away. If I was out driving and saw a school bus, a wave of strange, irrational anger would bubble up inside me. I would imagine crashing into it as if hitting the bus hard enough could somehow ease my pain.

Of course, I never acted on those thoughts, but they were there, raw and unrelenting. Even now, the sight of a school bus is difficult for me. I still find myself closing my eyes or looking away to avoid the memories and emotions it stirs up.

I put up a Christmas tree that year, trying to seem like I hadn't completely lost my mind. The grandkids would be coming over to open presents, and I wanted things to feel as normal as possible for them. I forced on a happy face, but inside I was trembling. All I could think about was wanting everyone to leave so I could retreat back to my broken, shattered self and stop pretending.

That was the last year I put up a big tree. Since 2010, I've only had a small tree, and that's enough for me.

The year 2011 had to get better. The unbearable pain and the constant desire to give up had to ease eventually. I have to admit, I was starting to feel a little better, but those relentless, crazy thoughts still lingered in my mind. This pain—how do I escape it? How do I get rid of this crushing weight that feels like it's tearing me apart from the inside?

January 11th, 2011

The school bus driver who ran my son over has once again been allowed a continuance from the Judge. His next scheduled appearance before the judge is February 3rd, 2011. Until that low life is behind bars, I will remain angry, I suppose. My anger cools, and then when I get this news once again, it fuels it all over again.

He killed my son on February 17th, 2010. Sadly, it has almost been a year, and this clown is still getting to spend time with his family and friends.

The system is messed up. If you have a vehicular homicide case against you -you should be first in line along with murder.

For the last few days, I feel like I am going crazy. I cry at everything. It has been almost a year, and I am experiencing anger all over again. I want to punch the wall, hit somebody, and crush everything on site. Keeping it all in is almost more than I can take. There is another: Call to Trial" on Friday, February 14th, and I am going. If the judge delays it again, I am going to speak up. Why does this asshole continue to be allowed to be with his family when he took away a part of mine. He needs to go to jail and miss his little girl like I miss my son, only it's not the same. I want to punch the guy. I am so angry right now. Lord help me!

My heart turned to stone. Vivid memories of Tripp would flood my mind, bringing both warmth and panic, until I was overwhelmed with the crushing realization that I couldn't go on without him. I avoided everyone, drowning in the unbearable intensity of my grief.

Deep down, I knew I had to keep going—I just didn't know how. All I wanted was to feel normal again, but what I truly wanted was my son back.

Then I had this brainstorm: I was going to turn it all around—stop grieving and start living again. It sounded simple enough in my head. Little did I know that grief doesn't come with an on-and-off switch.

February 13th, 2011-
A New Beginning after One Year of Absolute Misery

I have the best husband in the world. Today, as I was thinking, I realized just how much he has stood by me, even when I was at my lowest—teetering on the edge of despair. He has never tried to say the "right" thing or fix me. Instead, he has given me the space to cry, to grieve, and to simply be. He has never abandoned me through all my sorrow. He gives me alone time when I need it, never taking my distance personally. He is patient, kind, and endlessly loving.

He has supported me through every emotional storm, never trying to "fix" what cannot be fixed. He listens with an open heart, loves to talk about Tripp, and somehow loves me even more with each passing day. I love him so much, and so did Tripp.

My son always said Dan was his dad. Tripp never missed calling Dan on his birthday or Father's Day; when he was away at school, he would call just to talk or ask for advice.

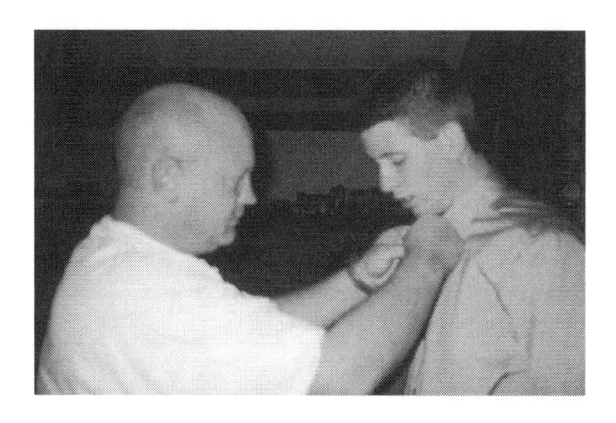

Why Me? - Navigating the Unbearable Truth of Grief and Loss

Today, I feel so grateful for my husband and the privilege of being Tripp's mom. Tripp was an incredible kid for 27 years, and I realize now—just four days away from his first angelversary—that it's time for me to start living again. I need to do this for Tripp because I know he would want me to. He loved life and lived it to the fullest—sometimes too much, if I'm being honest!

I'm making a choice today, right now, not to keep dying inside but to start living again. I carry beautiful memories of Tripp in my heart, and they will always be with me because no one can ever take them away. From now on, I choose to honor him by living positively and fully, just as he would want me to.

I didn't realize that making a promise to myself would be so difficult to keep. I learned no matter how many promises, I couldn't outrun the grief.

On February 17th, I'm going to celebrate. Celebrate a remarkable young man who brought me more joy than words could ever express. From the day he was born, Tripp filled my life with light. He didn't come into my life to bring me down or to be a source of pain, no matter what has happened. I can't change the fact that he's gone. He's no longer here on this earth, and that is something I will always grieve. But I can choose to step out of the darkness I've lived in this past year and move toward a healthier, more hopeful life.

I've asked "Why Me?" every single day, but I'm beginning to see how that only deepens my pain. Maybe the good Lord needed Tripp for something greater, or maybe his loss is meant to teach me to be a better person. I don't have the answers, but I do know this: I'm choosing to honor my son's legacy with love, joy, and gratitude.

I was bound and determined when I wrote that I was going to beat this grief thing. Ha.

The one-year date was approaching quickly, and I was torn about what to do. I live in Pennsylvania, but my son was buried in Arkansas, where we spent most of our life. He was killed here in Pennsylvania while living with me. I struggled with whether I should fly to Arkansas for that day or stay here and visit the scene of the crash.

I've never been someone who visits grave sites often because I believe his soul is in Heaven, and only his body rests there. Even though that's what I believe, I still don't know what the right choice is. In my heart, I think my son would prefer me to stay home, where I feel closest to him and where he last was with me.

I'm dreading that day as it is and just want to honor him in the best way I can. I keep thinking about the poem that says, *"Do not stand at my grave and weep, for I am not there."* It reminds me that he's with me no matter where I choose to be.

After the first year, I never felt the need to visit where he was buried or visit the crash site on that dreadful day because I always carried him close to me, no matter where I was. For anyone else facing the same dilemma, follow your heart and do whatever feels right for you—without guilt. There's no right or wrong way to grieve. Everyone processes loss and celebrates the life of their child in their own way. We all just learn as we go.

I'm sharing with you some of the things I experienced in the early years of my journey. I want to offer you a glimpse into my thoughts and the journey I've traveled.

On February 17th, 2011, a year after Tripp's passing, this is how I remembered my pain.

After Tripp was killed, I came to understand the true meaning of despair. My heart shattered into a million tiny pieces, leaving nothing but an empty shell inside me. Cries of disbelief echoed from my hollow soul, and the pain I felt was like a jagged knife cutting through the core of my being. I was so broken that my world stopped. When I fell to my knees screaming, I didn't want to get back up. I felt dead inside, and I couldn't comprehend how I was still breathing.

Why Me? - Navigating the Unbearable Truth of Grief and Loss

I stood in absolute darkness, knowing deep in my heart and spirit that I would never get better. My child was gone, and he wasn't coming back. The road ahead seemed certain to end in tragedy...

I truly didn't believe I would survive. Every day felt like a suffocating battle. I was consumed with endless tears and pain, pacing from room to room, searching for something—anything—to ease the agony. I cried out, *Why? Why me? Why my boy?* Why couldn't it be a bad person? Why couldn't it have been the bus driver or even Mike? Over and over, I begged God for help: *Do you even hear me?* Anger and grief intertwined as disbelief consumed me. My mind couldn't focus; I could barely function. I buried my face in Tripp's clothes several times a day, clinging to his scent as I wept hopelessly.

I was determined not to spend Tripp's first angelversary sitting around and crying. Dan wanted to stay home from work, but I told him I would be okay, and I decided to reach out to the friends I was supposed to have lunch with on the day Tripp was killed.

When I woke up that morning, I felt like I was being shielded again, as if something unseen was surrounding me. It reminded me of the beginning when nothing felt real. Driving to Cindy's felt strange, almost like someone else was behind the wheel. Still, I was determined to appear normal—or at least pretend to be normal. I got to Cindy, parked my car, and jumped in with her to ride over to meet the other gals. On the way, Cindy made one of those comments that stung more than helped. "I know how you feel," she said. "My brother died." I cut her off gently but firmly. "Cindy, stop. You don't know how I feel, and it's not the same." She paused and then admitted, "Well, I don't know because I don't have any children." I sighed. "Let's just not talk about it," I said, my eyes filling with tears. The rest of the drive was quiet, and I kept my emotions to myself.

At the restaurant, we had a great time together. I only cried a little, letting myself enjoy the moment as much as I could. But once we returned to Cindy's and I got back into my car, the tears began to fall. As I drove, the weight of it all came crashing down again. I had to pull over beside a lake.

Shirley Tripp Johnson

I sat there, letting the grief consume me. The tears poured from my eyes like waves, endless and uncontrollable. It felt as though the entire ocean had been waiting inside me, and now it was finally spilling out.

Once I managed to stop crying, I continued my drive home. Everything felt surreal like I was floating in a strange, hollow space, disconnected from the world. I stayed quiet for the rest of the evening, trying to hold myself together. I was determined not to write yet another sob story that evening on how I was feeling on Facebook—I didn't want to let the grief spill out there, too, but I did; then I sat with it, heavy and unrelenting, trying to navigate through another evening.

So many days, I thought I wouldn't make it through. Each moment felt unbearable like I was suffocating under the weight of my grief. Endless tears flowed as I paced aimlessly from room to room, searching for something—anything—that could ease the pain. I would

Why Me? - Navigating the Unbearable Truth of Grief and Loss

cry out, "Why? Why, my boy? God, help me!" I was so angry, consumed by the unfairness of it all.

After Tripp was killed, I learned that he had almost overdosed and was admitted to the hospital in Arkansas after his best friend was killed in a car accident. His friend Kara called to let me know he was there, but she made up something not serious and assured me there was no need for me to come to Arkansas. She said she would stay with him and that he would be okay. He had a wedding the next day, so he had to get better. I was completely shocked when I heard this after the fact. My heart broke all over again, imagining that my baby could have died and I wouldn't have been there for him.

This was written by Tripp when his best friend died.

I used this in his pamphlet at the funeral because it also described my boy.

> "No reason to dwell. Appreciate the memories that you got to share with such an indescribable one-of-a-kind human being.
>
> That's life; it only makes the strong STRONGER.
>
> To everyone, just appreciate the good times. – Tripp-

Chapter 4
Grief Speaks

When 2011 began, as usual, I found myself moving from the bed to the couch, still in my pajamas, when my daughter Deidre called one morning. She told me that her son, my grandson Landon, was having something at school, and he wanted me to come. I told her I can't—I just can't. Then she said, "Mom, I'm going to say something to you, and it's probably going to piss you off." I said, "Okay..." She then said, "We're not dead."

I sat in silence, letting her words sink in. Oh my God, what had I been doing? I felt this weight in my chest and thought, *What have I done?*

I told her, "I'll be there," and immediately went upstairs to take a shower. I headed over to Landon's event, and after that, I began to attend more of my grandkids' sports and school activities. I would sit there, tears flowing down my face, but I kept showing up.

I will never forget those words she said to me.

At that moment, I knew I had to make a change. I didn't know how, but I was determined to try. I had to. I had to start telling myself to live and push those dark thoughts out of my mind. I'd overcome so many challenges in my life already. This wasn't just another obstacle to conquer, but I knew I had to survive—and I would. I had to. I wanted to. I was going to. The pain was still there, but it was mine to carry, and I decided I'd take it with me and keep moving forward. I will survive.

In my desperation to find support, I opened Facebook and began to scroll and came across a group suggestion called Grieving Mothers. Immediately I requested to join, not knowing what I was about to find. I was accepted, and I began to read posts from moms sharing their experiences reading about the pain and sorrow of others who had lost a child. I realized I wasn't alone in my grief anymore. There was an entire world of grieving people out there that I never knew existed. Why hadn't anyone told me sooner? I was shocked reading what was being said about grief counselors. Counselors telling them to "get over it" or that "it's in the past." I couldn't believe anyone would say such things to a grieving mother. No! That is not how grief should be treated. A mother's loss isn't something you just "get over." It's a part of you forever.

After spending time reading about how grief-stricken moms were getting little to no help, I decided to go back to school to become a grief counselor. My goal was to help others while hopefully finding some healing for myself. I enrolled in an online program through The American Institute of Healthcare Professionals, specifically the Academy for Grief Counseling. Since I didn't have a healthcare degree, I had to jump through some hoops, but I finally got accepted. Determined to start helping as soon as possible, I threw myself into my studies, working day and night. I began the courses on April 22, 2011, and completed everything by November 8, 2011.

I thought the courses would teach me everything I needed to know about grief and how to get out of it. Boy, was I wrong? As I read through the chapters, it seemed they mostly lumped all types of grief together with only a few distinctions, many of which were not ringing true to me. Some of the material didn't make much sense to me at all after the loss of a child. I remember talking to my son Jeremiah, telling him that some chapters didn't seem to apply to grief at all. He replied, "Mom, you still have to study them because they'll be on the test." I laughed it off, thinking it didn't matter. But he was right. On my next test, I missed every question from those chapters and barely managed a C. That was a wake-up call—I made sure to pay attention after that!

I had set a goal to earn my certification, and I accomplished it.

One of the most valuable lessons I learned was that counseling isn't about giving advice—it's about listening. It's about providing a safe space for others to share their stories again and again, if needed, because through that process, healing slowly starts to creep in. It doesn't take the grief away, but it softens it, allowing you to breathe a little easier. It helps ease that crushing ache in your chest so you don't feel like your heart might give out from the pain.

After spending time in the Grieving Mothers Group and connecting with its creator, she suggested I start my group, and on May 1, 2011, *My Child Has Wings* was born. It became my refuge, a place where I could pour out my sorrow and connect with other grieving mothers who understood.

As the group grew, I noticed many people posting about the stages of grief, and some seemed confused. They couldn't understand why different people were at different stages, even if they had lost a child around the same time. One thing I learned during my grief counseling studies that stood out to me: the stages of grief, as outlined by Elisabeth Kübler-Ross, weren't originally written for those grieving the loss of a loved one.

Those stages—denial, anger, bargaining, depression, and acceptance—were developed to describe what *terminally ill patients* go through after being diagnosed with a life-ending illness. While someone grieving a death might experience some or all of these emotions, the stages were never intended to describe the grief process for those left behind after losing a child, parent, sibling, or friend.

Trying to explain this to the group was difficult because the concept of the "stages of grief" is so commonly—and loosely—used when someone dies. Many people had absorbed it as fact and found it hard to reconcile that their experiences didn't neatly fit into those stages. But grief is deeply personal, and there's no single roadmap for how it unfolds.

So much anger. Forgiveness—now that's a tough one, especially when someone has hurt your child. Whether it was through murder, an accident, or even mistreatment while they were alive, it feels impossible to let that anger go. After their death, we tend to cling to all of that pain, don't we? Blaming and shaming someone becomes a way to lash out to release some of our grief. But as we grieve, this need to hold onto anger will either get better or worse. That's why we have to start the forgiveness process so we can release the anger, or it will consume us.

The man who killed my son—I knew I had to forgive him because that's what the Lord tells us to do. But how? He killed my baby. I wrestled with that forgiveness for a long time. I realized that forgiving him didn't mean I was condoning what he did that day. It was about starting the process and releasing myself from the anger toward him. Forgiveness isn't a "once and done" kind of thing. It's ongoing. Even now, when those feelings creep back in, I have to remind myself to begin the process of forgiveness again. Forgiveness takes time, and it does not mean you forget what someone did.

Some people say they will never forgive someone who has wronged them. But holding on to that anger only allows it to fester and eat away at you for as long as you cling to it. It breeds bitterness, and personally, I choose not to live that way. Forgiveness is for our own peace, not the person who wronged us.

Starting that process can lift some of the weight off your shoulders. As grievers, we carry enough already; we don't need more weighing us down.

Consider this: forgiveness doesn't erase the past, but it can help you find a little peace as you move forward.

On May 29, 2011, I had my first dream where I could have sworn Tripp was standing right beside me. It felt so real that I called out his name when I woke up—but he was gone. I got out of bed and immediately wrote down what he said to me in the dream. This is what he told me:

> **Dear Mom,**
>
> You dreamed of me last night, and what I said was true, I may not be with you here on earth, but I am still with you. You took my hand and asked me if I was truly gone, and I smiled at you and said, no, Mom, you are not alone. I am always right here with you through all your

pain and grief; my prayer for you each day is to somehow find relief. I know how much you love me, Mom, and you think of me all the time; just know that I am ok, and I will see you again one day. Remember, with each new dawn, I am not gone.

I love you, Mom.

Have you ever received signs from your child? If you have, it's such an incredible feeling—one that brings love, comfort, and reassurance. If you haven't, don't lose hope. Stay open to even the smallest details. Signs can come in many forms—a dream, something in the skies or nature, or even a meaningful song. Pay attention and affirm to yourself that if they can reach out to you, they will. Stay open, stay aware, and keep looking.

Now for a few of my 2011 random thoughts and emotions that I posted in my group in my second year in grief. When I believed something would help, I would post it in my group to help others while I was trying to help myself. I truly believe that we were healing together.

July 21st, 2011

-What moves through us is a silence, a quiet sadness, a longing for one more day, one more word, one more touch, we may not understand why you left this earth so soon or why you left before we were ready to say goodbye, but little by little, we begin to remember not just that you died, but that you lived. And that your life gave us memories too beautiful to forget.

July 29th, 2011

Losing a child is like being in a broken-down car. Looking back feels unbearable, filled with painful memories, while moving forward seems impossible without them. So, we remain in neutral, gripping the emergency brake tightly, hoping that one day we'll find the strength to move again.

Make a decision that, from this moment on, you will never be less than friendly toward yourself.
No more treating yourself like a slave.
No more putting yourself down - ever.
No more negative assumptions.
No more torment over past events that you can't change.
No more "putting up with" other people's abuse or unkindness.
No more postponing doing what you love most.
This will radically change the way you feel on the inside. It will change the way that you think about other people, interpret their behavior, respond to them, and act toward them.

It is impossible to see the world as a friendly place (despite the disappointments and hassles) until the world inside your own mind is also friendly.

When the old thoughts or behaviors arise, see them for what they are (tired, useless habits) and move on. They will continue to tug at you, but only as long as you pay attention.

June 29, 2011

Who is it that I need to forgive? The answer is everyone.

I must start by forgiving myself for anything I have done wrong. Whether it's not offering love when it is needed, not being supportive, or creating negativity in my own life or someone else's, I must let go of the weight I've been carrying. I also need to forgive others—But how do you forgive and stop holding onto the past?

Take everything I've been through and allow it to empower me. I can't change the past, but I can discover something of value within it. When I do, I'll find the ability to forgive both myself and others. I won't carry the burdens of the past any longer—I'll be free.

June 30th, 2011

I'm tired of pretending I'm okay when I'm not.

I'm tired of faking a smile when all I wanna do is cry.

Shirley Tripp Johnson

I'm tired of pretending I can live without you when I'm dying without you.

I'm tired of pretending I can laugh without friends when I need them.

I'm tired of pretending I have a perfect life when my life is a mess.

I'm tired of believing I can when I can't.

I'm just tired of becoming someone else who isn't me.

July 31st, 2011

This photo shows my son Tripp (on the right) playing his harmonica. My grandson Landon always visits Tripp's room when he stays with us, going through all of Tripp's belongings—every time. On this occasion, he picked up the harmonica, went out to the front porch, and began to play. I cried so hard. It was a mix of happiness and deep sadness. Tripp loved Landon so much, and it breaks my heart to know that Landon's memories of him will be limited to just nine years. They would have made such a great team together.

I ended up photo-shopping a picture of the two of them playing together. The neighbors all commented on how beautifully Landon played. It was as if, when he closed his little eyes, he was somewhere else... or maybe Tripp was there with him.

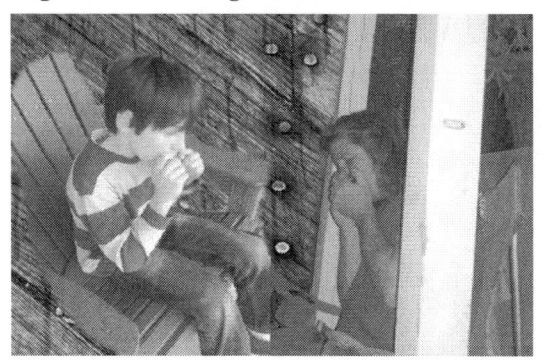

A deep sadness fills me when I see this photo. Landon loved his Uncle Tripp so much, and now he'll never get to experience the fun with "TrippNAintEZ" again.

Why Me? - Navigating the Unbearable Truth of Grief and Loss

August 7th, 2011

Discovering a letter your child wrote to you after their passing can hold profound significance. It serves as a tangible reminder of their love, memories, and unique personality, offering comfort during a time when you may feel distant from them. This letter allowed me to hear Tripp's voice again, even in his absence, and can be an essential part of the grieving process, helping you revisit precious moments and expressions of their affection.

> Mom
>
> Hello just thought I would write you a little note telling you how much I love you and appreciate everything you do for me.
>
> Love you tons
> TRIPP

Clinging to their clothes, phone, or any belongings is a natural response for a grieving mother after the loss of a child. In the first year, their scent lingers, bringing a bittersweet comfort, but as the smell fades, it can feel like losing them all over again. In truth, every day feels like a new loss as the reality of their absence dawns anew each morning. The day your child passes becomes etched into your heart and mind forever—an indelible mark of love and pain.

It's important to honor every memory. Walk down memory lane often. Bring out the photos, let the tears flow freely, and embrace the grief. Healing comes in waves, carried by the ocean of tears we shed. Each tear is a step toward healing—a testament to the depth of our love

Shirley Tripp Johnson

August 14th, 2011

God doesn't have a Blackberry or an iPhone, but He's still my favorite contact. He doesn't have Facebook, but He's my closest friend. He doesn't have Twitter, but I follow Him wholeheartedly. He doesn't need the internet, yet I'm always connected to Him. And the best part? His communication line is always open—no waiting, no holding music, just Him.

August 17th, 2011

Eighteen months ago today, we lost our Tripp. No more family photos, no more big hugs, no more of his infectious laugh or hearing him say, "It's a beautiful day, Mama." No more phone calls just to check in... no more smelling his cologne as he bounced down the stairs. No more buying cereal by the boatload, no more hearing him say, "I love you, Mama." Just... no more.

September 17, 2011

Nineteen months ago today, my life changed forever.

I awake from sleep, remembering going downstairs and finding you romancing your cereal in a dimly lit room. Not saying a word, I smile, knowing it is your "alone" time. A few hours later, you awake with a big smile, ready to begin your day, and with a hug and a kiss, you drive away on a snowy, cloudy day, never to return.

I love you, son, more than words can express. I miss you so much. Remembering the joy, you brought to me while you were here leaves me aching with tears running down my face. I never knew how much I loved you until I lost you. You were a light. You brightened my life. I try and stay strong because I know you would want me to but I am weak today. If you can pull a favor for me on this day and ask the Lord to send me strength, I would be grateful because, for some reason.... today.......seems like nineteen months ago.

September 19th, 2011

A Native American grandfather sits with his young grandson and shares a lesson. "Inside each of us, there are two wolves in a constant battle," he says. "One wolf represents peace, love, and kindness. The other stands for fear, greed, and hatred."

The boy thinks for a moment and asks, "Which wolf will win, Grandfather?"

The grandfather smiles gently and replies, "The one you feed."

Which one are you feeding? This is a question we all need to ask ourselves. If we continue to feed resentment and anger, they will only grow and fester within us. Instead, we must choose to feed the positive. Turn away from negative thoughts when they arise.

I understand that some people are naturally more negative, but it *can* be changed. When a negative thought enters your mind, don't feed it—stop and shift your focus to something positive, something that brings you joy or peace.

We can't afford to hold onto negativity and refuse to let it go. It weighs us down, crushes our spirit, and makes the process of grieving even more difficult. Letting go and feeding the positive will help lighten that burden and allow healing to begin.

October 2nd, 2011

Experiencing the loss of a loved one is profoundly challenging. During such times, it's essential to have a support system that understands and respects your needs. Here's a heartfelt message you might consider sharing with those around you:

Don't avoid me—tragedy isn't contagious. If you feel uncomfortable because you don't know what to say, just hug me and let me know you care. Please be patient with my moods. There will be times when nothing anyone says or does feels right, but I need to know that my grumpiness or sadness won't push you away and that you'll keep showing up to support me. If you ask how I'm doing, be ready to truly listen. When I'm hurting, I need someone willing to hear me out and let me share my pain.

October 12th, 2011

Need to Borrow a Cup of Courage? When you're down and out, sometimes you need to borrow the courage to move forward. Once you do, a time may come when someone else needs it — and you can pay it forward.

October 14th, 2011

When our child dies, our world crashes. Life stops as we once knew it, and it is never the same again. One of the most painful things to bereaved parents is watching the rest of the world move on just as though nothing ever happened. They just don't get it.

Why Me? - Navigating the Unbearable Truth of Grief and Loss

December 9th, 2011 - I wrote this poem

The Holidays are upon us, and we feel sadness and fear

Our child is no longer with us, and we just want them near.

We remember joy and cheer from all the years past

And how each Christmas Day we always had a blast.

The time leading up to this spectacular day

It should be filled with joy and lots of child play.

As we hang the ornaments on the tree

A special one is placed at the top by me.

As tears roll from my eyes, missing you with all my heart

I suddenly feel peace and know we are not apart.

Your spirit is with me even though you're not here

Smiling upon the family that you loved so dear.

You sent me a message in a dream last night

To remember your life and your smile so bright.

Remembering to live life as I always did

Loving and giving and being a kid.

Be joyous during this Christmas season.

Always remember, there is a reason.

Keep me close in your heart today and every day

Always knowing that I love you in every way.

Live your life to the fullest with each moment you are given

For you don't know what is next on the roads that are driven.

Enjoy the Holiday with bliss and cheer

Embrace our Family and know I am near.

Take the family pictures as you always do

Shirley Tripp Johnson

I am smiling and goofing off as I think of you.

I know you won't forget me as long as you breathing

So, live your life, my dear Mom, and stop all that grieving.

If I could take away all of your pain

I would in a moment so you wouldn't feel insane.

I am happy, Mom, it's great up here

I look forward to seeing you when your time draws near.

I will meet you with the biggest hug of all

And you will then know why I didn't have time to call.

I thought I would throw that in and hope to see you smile

I remember when you missed my calls when it had been a while.

I love you, Mama, always have and always will

You were always there for me even when I was being a pill.

I know each tear you shed and the pain within your heart

But please always remember, we're not apart.

I know it doesn't seem sometimes that I am close and near

But I am holding you, Mom, catching your every tear.

Please enjoy your Christmas day with the family who love you so much

Just be careful because I might spike the punch.

Know I love you, and watch for signs that I am there

And as always, we lift our moms in prayer.

Enjoy the season and the day

I'll be taking a ride in Santa's Sleigh

Merry Christmas Mom

~Shirley Tripp Johnson~

December 9th, 2011

The leaves shimmer as the wind begins to whisper in the night. The air fills with fury as the storm approaches closer, and the weaker branches begin to break. The branches have become weak from lack of nourishment or from a child swinging happily, but the trunk remains and is planted sternly beneath the earth, the roots, the main source of strength. As the fierce winds blow, the strong remains and always produces new branches in the hope of strength before the next wind. Stand tall and be strong, for life is like a tree, and the storms continue through our growth and are not always pleasing. Only a foundation will help us survive, so always use that foundation for everything you do. We can't give up. We must keep growing- even though our branches become dry and brittle and sometimes break. The road is always uphill. Sure, we get on even ground at times, but only to find the next hill is steeper to climb. Never fear; we have to be in the valley before traveling to the peak.

What moves through us is a silence, a quiet sadness, a longing for one more day, one more word, one more touch, we may not understand why you left this earth so soon or why you left before we were ready to say goodbye, but little by little, we begin to remember not just that you died, but that you lived. And that your life gave us memories too beautiful to forget. ~ author unknown

December 14th, 2011

TODAY, I WILL CHOOSE JOY. There is so much sorrow all around us, especially as the Christmas season draws near. We remember yesteryears and days gone by. We remember our child that is gone too soon from our arms no matter what their age and no matter the time we were given with them. There comes a time when we must make a choice to cross over the extreme pain and allow our broken hearts to begin to heal. When we allow the joy to enter our hearts-little by little it will begin to root out the pain that stabs us with every breath we take. We can find joy in memories. We can find joy remembering their smile, we can find joy just remembering their presence. We can find joy in looking at a photo. We can find joy by remembering past Holidays and the cheer it brought to them. We can find joy in almost anything if we allow ourselves. We can find joy through our tears. Joy does not mean we are letting our child go because we would never do that. Joy helps us to cherish their memory in a different light. We will grieve until the day we die because of the love we have for our child, but we can learn to grieve with joy in our hearts. Try to find JOY today, even if it is only for a moment. Allow Joy to be a part of your life while you cherish those unforgettable memories of your child. Allow joy and laughter to be a part of your life. What Joy can you find today?

December, 2011

Have you ever heard the song,

"I've got joy joy joy joy down in my heart, down in my heart. down in my heart. I've got joy joy joy joy down in my heart to stay."? For many of us, finding joy seems to be a far reach after our child dies. Think about this for a moment. Joy resides in our hearts, and now that our child has died, they remain in our hearts. If our love for our child and joy resides in the same place (our hearts), then yes, one day, we can dust off the sorrow that has our joy nestled in a dark corner of our hearts. Our children are our joy in life and even in death. The sadness is overwhelming, but once we begin to try and accept our child is not coming back and the time, we had with them is just what it was, then we can begin to find our joy again. The joy our child brought us for many years, months, days, or hours will always remain in our hearts. At some point on this journey (time unknown), we want our joy back. We want to be able to smile when we walk down memory lane and remember the joyful and not-so-joyful times we experienced with our children. Every day, my son would say, "It's a beautiful day, Mom". It didn't matter if it was hot, cold, dry, or wet; he lived each day to the fullest and always with a smile on his face. I miss him so much, but he was my joy for 27 years, and now, in death, he is my joy. No one can take that joy away from me or you. Tears accompany joy, so don't ever think because you cry, you don't have joy. For those of you who have just begun this journey.... smile when you can, for that is joy, even though right now it doesn't feel like it.

Why Me? - Navigating the Unbearable Truth of Grief and Loss

Don't feel guilty for laughing or having a good day. Finding our new normal takes years, and I am convinced of that, but along the way, we still carry all the love for our children. We are their memory keeper forever and ever as long as we live. They now reside in our hearts, curled up with joy. Just for today.... look for joy. Grab it. Hold on to it and smile, knowing that joy is your child. It may be a butterfly, a song, a sweet baby smiling or just a friendly face......smile back. It's called JOY!

Those were some of the little thoughts I posted in my group. I could already tell that starting my group and sharing with other grievers was helping me. Instead of wanting to die, I was trying to save others who wanted to. Members would post that they were giving up and wanted to end it. It broke my heart because I had once felt that way myself.

We had several moms in the group who did take their own lives because the pain was too much to bear. I understood their pain, but I knew now that we could make it past those feelings, but it was much work and taking one moment at a time and trying to change that thought pattern. It is not easy. My children and my husband saved me and they didn't even know it.

When I was in my darkest moments, what I wished for most was someone who truly understood what I was feeling—someone who had been there. But I didn't have that, and it made the struggle so much harder.

Shirley Tripp Johnson

Starting my group made me realize how much something like this was needed. If I'd had a supportive space like that back then, I might not have carried those heavy thoughts for so long.

Chapter 5

Shattered by Grief

In this moment of deep despair, it might be impossible to recognize the wisdom within the grief process. Only with time and reflection will you see how it gently carried you forward, offering exactly what you needed, precisely when you needed it.

The message for you now is clear: trust the process of grief. As excruciating as it feels, grief is not your enemy—it's a guide that will, in time, lead you back to life.

There is no loss as profound as that of a child. Others may try to identify with their own experiences of loss, attempting to be helpful. However, it often feels like no one can truly understand the depth of your pain unless they have endured the death of a child themselves. These well-meaning gestures, while offered with kindness, may feel hollow or even frustrating.

It can seem impossible that anyone could grasp the weight of this grief. Yet, the truth remains that most people will encounter profound sorrow at some point in their lives. Many emerge from these experiences with resilience and without lasting harm. Like them, you cannot avoid the transformative journey that Sigmund Freud once described as the "work of mourning." It is a process that reshapes you, requiring time, patience, and compassion for yourself.

A Letter from Grief

> I come to you without words, yet every person and every land knows me. I weigh heavy on your chest, fog your mind, and leave a hollow ache in your heart. I am

the constant reminder of what is gone—the gaping void left by someone you loved deeply. I am the invisible presence, wreaking havoc with your thoughts, turning even the sunniest day into ruins.

You cannot escape me. I move in silence, loud only to the one I visit, forcing you to walk through life as if I am not there. I am a scrapbook of memories, an unwanted guest who lingers. You push me away, bury me beneath forced smiles and busy days, but I remain, hiding in the corners of your mind, whispering their name in quiet moments. I resurface in echoes of laughter that once filled your world, unearthing the volcano of emotions buried deep within you.

I come in waves—sometimes a sudden torrent, crashing over you with unbearable sorrow, leaving you gasping for air. Other times, I am a dull, persistent ache, your unwelcome companion. I hold up fragments of your pain, anger, and disbelief, forcing you to face the depth of your loss. I thrive on your emotions, trusting your memory to fuel my purpose, and I rarely find it lacking.

You may resent me, blame me, or blame yourself. You may search endlessly for what could have been done differently. But know this: I am not your enemy. I am the consequence of love, proof of the deep connection you shared. In the beginning, I am relentless. I invade your dreams with vivid images, turning sweet moments into haunting nightmares. I whisper lies that life is no longer worth living. But even as I torment, my purpose is not to destroy.

My role is difficult yet necessary, like that of an undertaker—unwanted but vital. I am here to guide you through grief, a process as painful as it is essential. The work of mourning is hard, and only you can do it. Yet, through this work comes transformation. Over time, my sharp edges will soften. The unbearable weight of pain will shift into gentler memories—smiles, whispers, and love will replace horror.

Let me stay as long as you need me. I promise to step back when it becomes too much and return only when you call. I know my role well, and I am here to help you navigate the road ahead. Embrace the tears, lean on those around you, and trust that this process, though grueling, is a testament to the love you still carry. In time, you will find a way to carry that love forward, not as a burden but as a source of strength.

Your Friend, Grief

Does that sound familiar? I'm sure it does. Grief can feel like it's going to break us, but it doesn't have to.

Unrelenting grief is a profound, all-encompassing sorrow that seems to have no end. It is a weight that presses against the chest, a constant ache that permeates every moment, awake or asleep. This type of grief resists the passage of time and the solace of well-meaning words. It can feel like an endless loop, where each day begins with the same raw pain as the day before. You may feel like you can't go on another day with such an unbearable crushing pain shattering your every move.

The world continues to move forward, but for the person enduring unrelenting grief, time feels frozen. Thoughts repeatedly return to the source of their loss, replaying memories, "what-ifs," and unresolved longings. The simplest tasks become monumental challenges as the burden of sorrow drains energy and motivation.

Emotionally, it may manifest as waves of sadness, anger, guilt, or despair, often without warning. Physically, it can bring exhaustion, loss of appetite, or a heavy fatigue that no amount of rest can seem to alleviate. It's as though the person grieving is carrying an invisible wound that never heals.

Unrelenting grief also isolates, making it feel as if no one can truly understand the depth of the pain. Even among loved ones, a sense of

Why Me? - Navigating the Unbearable Truth of Grief and Loss

being profoundly alone in the experience can take hold, amplifying feelings of despair. Yet, despite its intensity, even the most unyielding grief has moments—however fleeting—of relief, signaling the potential for healing in time. Grab them.

I know it's hard to take the first step, but I believe one of the most important things a grieving parent can do is join a Facebook group for parents who have lost a child. In my opinion, this can provide invaluable support. You might need to try a few groups before finding one that truly fits, as the tone and responses in each group can vary greatly. Not all child loss groups are the same.

I recommend joining a closed, general group that welcomes parents from all types of loss experiences. These spaces can offer incredible insight and understanding as you hear stories from a diverse range of parents. Limiting yourself to groups focused only on specific types of loss may prevent you from learning from the broader spectrum of shared grief.

Yes, you will hear many heartbreaking stories, but your story is just as sad and significant as any other parent's. Never let anyone make you feel like your loss is less important or unworthy of support. Every loss matters, and in these groups, you'll find people who truly understand the depth of your pain.

I want to share with you why I feel this way. Early in my journey, I attended a Compassionate Friends meeting. During one session, a woman arrived late and took the last available seat. As we went around the circle, each person sharing their story of loss, the room was heavy with tears and grief.

Two women in the group spoke about their children being killed by drunk drivers. Through their anguish, they expressed their anger, saying they hoped the families of the drunk drivers would rot in hell. I was appalled by such cruel words, though I understood it was their pain speaking.

When it was finally the latecomer's turn to share, she suddenly got up, sobbing uncontrollably, and left the room. Concerned, I followed her out to ask what was wrong. Through her tears, she told me she didn't think she could ever come back. Her story was different: one night, her son left a bar drunk, drove head-on into another car, and was killed. Tragically, one person in the other car also died. Her son had been that drunk driver.

I felt so deeply for her. I tried to console her, assuring her that no matter the circumstances, she deserved support because she, too, had lost a child. I explained that some people speak from a place of intense anger and grief, and their words don't always reflect how they truly feel as time softens their pain.

With encouragement, she agreed to return to the room with me. As we walked back in, all eyes turned toward us, and the group leader welcomed her back. She had calmed herself enough to share her story. As she spoke, the expressions of shock and remorse on the other parents' faces were palpable. One by one, they began to apologize, explaining they never meant to hurt her.

This experience taught me a profound lesson. Some parents lose children under circumstances that involve mistakes or wrongdoing, but those parents didn't cause it. They are grieving, too, and should never be judged for their child's actions. Compassion should always prevail.

Sharing your story repeatedly is a crucial part of the healing process. While some people may say they don't want to talk about it, and that's their choice, holding in such profound grief can take a heavy emotional toll. Bottling up feelings can intensify anger, guilt, or other emotions, making them harder to manage over time.

That's why I believe it's essential to connect with others who have experienced the loss of a child. Whether it's meeting in person, talking on the phone, or participating in online groups, finding those who truly understand can provide comfort and support.

When I first started my Facebook group, I would post questions asking members where they were from, hoping to connect with people who lived within driving distance. Over time, I saw beautiful friendships form—not just through in-person meetings but also through phone conversations. I'll never forget the joy I felt when I

Why Me? - Navigating the Unbearable Truth of Grief and Loss

received my first message from two members in Tennessee who had met for lunch after finding each other through the group. Their names are Melanie and Roberta, and I am blessed to have met both of these ladies and spent time with them. Melanie has become a dear friend of mine, and we meet up and spend time together.

These connections remind us that even in the darkest times, we are not alone, and others truly understand the depth of our pain.

In the first couple of years, it's hard to comprehend that grief is an expression of the deep love we have for the child who died. Over time, we come to realize that grief is love turned inside out.

Life, once vibrant and colorful, suddenly shifts to stark black and white, eventually fading into muted shades of gray. We begin to wonder if we'll ever experience the vivid colors of joy and beauty again.

Grief is agony—a relentless tsunami that crashes into our emotions with unimaginable force, dragging us into the darkest depths. It wreaks havoc on our mind, body, and soul, leaving no part of us untouched.

Grief plays cruel games with our minds. It sneaks in uninvited, bringing haunting images, overwhelming guilt, and a relentless wave of raw emotions. There's no escaping its grip.

Grief does not discriminate. No one is immune to its power. We may try to suppress it, but unacknowledged grief will grow stronger, suffocating us from within until we are broken into countless pieces. It forces its way into every corner of our being, driving us through intense pain, searing anger, and profound disbelief.

Grief carves deep valleys of sorrow, whispering despair and tempting us to believe that life is no longer worth living. It's natural to question why grief strikes so mercilessly, especially at a parent who has lost a child.

When the weight becomes unbearable, grief may retreat for a moment, offering a fleeting reprieve. But before we know it, it returns with the force of a roaring lion, ready to consume us once more. Yet, as cruel as grief feels, it is also a guide.

Grief forces us to confront our pain, demanding the hard work of processing our loss. It is both a tormentor and a teacher, helping us navigate the long, arduous journey of healing. As painful as it is, we cannot begin to take the first steps toward healing without the help of grief itself.

Throughout life, we often hear the phrase "good grief" used as an exclamation of irritation, frustration, or surprise. Isn't that ironic? For many of us early in our grief journey, the idea of "good" and "grief" being connected seems impossible. "There's nothing good about grief," we think.

However, one thing we must confront is the danger of delayed grief. This isn't the same as denial. Delayed grief occurs when you push your pain aside, refusing to feel or work through it. You might be someone who bottles everything up, appearing fine on the surface but becoming irritable, resentful, or even angry as those suppressed emotions quietly eat away at you.

Don't be fooled into thinking you can avoid grief forever. Those emotions will eventually resurface, often with greater intensity. When they do, it can feel overwhelming—far worse than if you had faced them when they first appeared.

It's important to remember that you don't have to appear strong all the time. Experiencing grief doesn't make you weak. Grief requires courage—a profound kind of bravery that strengthens you as you walk this difficult path. It takes courage to face the pain, to allow yourself to feel it fully, and to begin the process of healing.

Lean into that courage. Allow yourself to release what you've held inside. Holding your emotions hostage doesn't make them disappear—it only forces them to find another way to escape. Permit yourself to express your feelings through tears, words, memories, or conversations about your child. By doing so, you'll begin to lighten the emotional burden and honor your grief in a way that fosters healing.

Why Me? - Navigating the Unbearable Truth of Grief and Loss

I remember about four years into my grief journey; I called a friend who had lost her son a few years before me. I told her something strange was happening—I was beginning to remember things I hadn't thought about in years. Past events I thought I'd let go of were suddenly resurfacing, and I found myself haunted by unresolved emotions.

She explained that this was a natural part of the grieving process. Grief, she said, has a way of unearthing anything unresolved, forcing us to confront it. At first, I found that hard to accept. On top of grieving my son, I now had to face these buried feelings. I had to work on myself, which felt overwhelming. I had to address guilt, shame, forgiveness, and the emotional baggage from my past.

It wasn't easy. At times, it was deeply upsetting and exhausting, but I did the work. Even now, something small may creep back in—an old memory or unresolved feeling—and when it does, I know what I need to do.

None of us are perfect, and while these things may not always relate directly to the loss of our child, they're part of the transformation that happens after such a devastating experience. It's like being broken apart and pieced back together, little by little. Grief isn't just about mourning; it's about becoming.

It's as though God is pulling us by our roots and giving us a cleansing bath, sending us back to face our struggles again and again until we're finally free of the weight that holds us back. Each step of this journey is part of building a new version of ourselves—a version shaped by love, loss, and healing.

On this grief journey, it's important to openly express your feelings. Seek support from others and consider joining an online grief group. In these groups, you'll find a judgment-free space to share your emotions with people who truly understand.

Allow yourself to fully experience the pain you feel. Be honest about your grief with friends and family. Most importantly, try to connect with other parents who have experienced losses. Building these relationships can be incredibly comforting because they allow for openness and honesty without fear of being misunderstood.

Some people approach grief as a problem to be solved, often trying to find logical ways to cope. Fathers, in particular, may lean toward this approach and sometimes hesitate to openly express their emotions, preferring private conversations instead. Some mothers may also grieve this way.

It's essential to remember that everyone grieves differently. We should never judge someone else's way of coping, even if it doesn't align with our own. While we may share the common bond of loss, every person's life and experiences are unique. It's only by taking the time to know one another that we can fully understand and support each other on this difficult journey.

My group will be listed in the back section of this book, so if you're looking for a closed group on Facebook, I'd be glad to have you join us.

However, I strongly advise one important thing: be cautious about the type of group you join online. Make sure the group is **closed**, not public. In public groups, anyone can see what you post, which can lead to unwanted exposure.

I've had people reach out to me, devastated because a family member saw something they posted. This happened because they were in a public group where all posts were visible. If you prefer to keep your feelings and emotions private, always ensure you're joining a **closed group** where only members can see what's shared.

Your privacy is important, and taking the extra step to protect it can make all the difference as you navigate your grief journey.

I wish there were some magical words or a quick fix that could make us all feel better, but there are just no words.

As the years go by, I miss my son, Tripp, more and more each day. The intense, raw pain may soften with time, but the emptiness, the yearning, only deepens.

Why Me? - Navigating the Unbearable Truth of Grief and Loss

For those of you who are new to this journey, my heart breaks for you. It's a path filled with confusion and heartache, one that changes as time passes, yet one thing remains unchanged: the love we have for our children.

As I wrote earlier, People may say things that unintentionally hurt us. They might try to connect by sharing their own experiences—whether it's the loss of a pet, a cousin, a friend, or even a parent—but the truth is, there is no comparison. We understand this, even if they don't. It's essential not to let those words cut too deep. People are simply trying to relate in their own way, even if they don't fully grasp the depth of our grief. They are merely trying to understand the pain they have felt with their loss, but they have no clue when they say it; it gives us no comfort. The only comforting words of understanding can only come from another parent who truly does understand.

When someone says, "I can't imagine," my response is always the same: "If you can't imagine it, then I can't explain it because it's truly unimaginable."

Grief is love turned inside out. It's not something we can simply turn off. We can't stop loving those we've lost. The pain we feel comes from that deep love, and it's a burden we bear because someone we cherished with all our hearts is no longer here. But they will always live in our hearts, and one day, we will see them again.

The loss of a child is intensely personal, and it's no one's place to tell us how we should grieve or how long it should take to begin to heal. It's like offering someone a single tissue when they truly need an entire box.

Believe it or not, life goes on after a funeral, but for us, it doesn't feel that way. It's so unfair. Life moves forward for everyone else while we're left stuck in time, trying to navigate a world without one of our children. People may mean well, but they don't truly understand. Don't set expectations for them because, in the end, it's only you who will be disappointed. I know this from experience, and many of you know it, too.

Shirley Tripp Johnson

It was Tripp's fourth angelversary, and my daughter, Deidre, my son, Jeremiah, and one of Tripp's best friends seemed to not acknowledge the day or say anything to me on February 17th, 2014. In a wave of anger, I sent them all a message, shaming them for not expressing anything. The following morning, I received messages from Deidre and Jeremiah, both saying similar things. They explained that they didn't like remembering that horrible day, but they would always honor Tripp's birthday and apologize for unintentionally hurting me. After reading their messages, I felt awful and immediately apologized. I won't share something so personal from them, But I do want to share the heartfelt message I received from Tripp's best friend. His words helped me understand how grief affects everyone differently:

> *"Unfortunately, for people like you, those who've experienced a loss so profound that others may never understand, grief manifests in ways that seem selfish or insensitive. Often, we think we're honoring the person we've lost, but we fail to realize that our actions—or inactions—can unknowingly add to the pain of those grieving. At the time of Tripp's passing, I was a young man in my 20s, still figuring out how to cope with the loss of my closest friend. I might have distanced myself from people and situations, and in doing so, I likely hurt you.
>
> I thought I had to be tough, that showing emotion or grief to someone who had lost their child would be selfish. I was afraid, not knowing how to share my pain with you. In hindsight, I realize that was foolish and naïve, and I hope you can forgive me. I never meant to hurt you. Tripp was one of my closest friends, and I will always remember him and the memories we shared. I will continue to visit his grave, and his memory will always live on in my life." *

Why Me? - Navigating the Unbearable Truth of Grief and Loss

I was moved by his honesty and vulnerability. His message helped me see that not everyone knows how to navigate grief, and sometimes, people unintentionally distance themselves because they're unsure of how to support others. His words also reminded me that Tripp's memory is cherished by more than just me, and that brings some comfort.

The following day, I responded with my apology.

> **"Thank you. I'm so sorry for the anger I expressed. After I wrote it, I realized how selfish I was being by expecting others to grieve or remember in the way I wanted. Grief is a complex, difficult emotion, and I understand that it affects each of us differently. Please know I miss Tripp deeply, and every day without him is incredibly painful. I am broken, but I appreciate you sharing your memories and honoring him."**

What his friend shared with me that day reminds me of the importance of compassion and understanding, especially in the face of grief. We all carry the weight of loss in different ways, and it's crucial to remember that even those who may seem distant or detached might be grieving in their own silent, personal way. And in the end, we all miss the ones we love—those who have left us too soon.

The black hole. You know it all too well. It's that place where you feel completely bottomed out—dark, suffocating darkness. You can't seem to stop the emotions, and you retreat into that hole, shivering with fear, trembling in despair. You feel like you'll never see the light again and feel you can't go on at times.

But here's the good news: you will. Yes, believe it or not, you will. We all fall into that black hole during the grief process, and it's where much of our healing takes place. It may feel impossible to imagine, but within that darkness, there is growth and healing taking place. That hole is where we come to terms with much stuff, both good and bad. As you move through your grief, you may find yourself in that hole over and over again. It's not a place to stay, though.

Shirley Tripp Johnson

Do the work you must do while you're there—scared, uncertain, and determined. The time you spend there will vary. There is no set time limit. It's important to know that as you move through it, you must eventually begin to look up. Slowly, the light will reappear. And as it does, you'll begin to rise again, inch by inch.

Once you fall into the hole, there is no way out of it but up, and when you get back to the peak, you will feel a sense of renewal. It might not be much, especially in the beginning, but you will finally notice a difference when you rise back up. Each time you go there, you are learning, you are growing, and you are healing. That black hole will also be the place that reminds you of all your wrongdoings.... Go with it-Do what you've got to do. It might mean forgiving someone or yourself, letting go of guilt and shame, etc.

Once you reach the top, you will find moments of joy. Don't feel guilty about trying to find joy early in your grief. It may not last long in the beginning, and you may feel conflicted, but it's okay. Grab onto that joy when it appears, even if it's just for a fleeting moment. Anything that makes you smile or turns your lip up, no matter how small, is a form of joy. Don't let it slip away. It may quickly turn into tears in the early stages, but that's okay too. Joy and sorrow often coexist. Let yourself have both.

If you're struggling in the beginning stages of your grief, or if you're still finding it difficult to accomplish anything, I recommend writing down the things you need to do the night before. I still do this myself. It helps me stay focused, and I cross off each task as I complete it.

In the early days, you might only be able to write down a couple of things like "get out of bed" or "brush your teeth," and that's okay. As you move through your grief journey, start adding one small productive task, like taking a shower or loading or unloading the dishwasher. Gradually, it can help you feel a sense of accomplishment, even on the hardest days.

Our minds are often too foggy in the beginning to focus on what needs to be done because we don't feel like doing anything at all. And if you're forgetful like me, it becomes even more important. I still

Why Me? - Navigating the Unbearable Truth of Grief and Loss

write a list every night before I go to bed, even fifteen years later. My memory used to be so bad that someone once joked I had CRS, "Can't Remember Shit." Later, it became "CRAFT". "Can't Remember a F***ing Thing." If you struggle with this, I get it. That's why having a list can make such a difference.

Looking back, I wish someone had come to me and prepared me for what I was about to face. Maybe if I'd had some kind of knowledge or guidance, I would have approached it all differently. That's one of the main reasons I wanted to help others. It doesn't have to be about facing every day wanting to give up—there is light to be found as you move through the journey. I just wish someone, anyone, had come to me and told me how dark and overwhelming it would get before it started to improve. Instead, I let it consume me. Having that kind of guidance and understanding could have made all the difference in how I navigated those early days and years of grief.

We had just hidden from Landon. He was about to come around the corner, and we were going to scare him. If I remember correctly, he just started laughing at us all huddled down on the floor, looking goofy.

Chapter 6

Finding My Way Back to Joy

My two-year mark is fast approaching. It's hard to believe so much time has passed without a hug, a kiss, that contagious smile, or Tripp's sense of humor. I miss him more every day, and with each passing day comes a new wave of tears. I still find myself shaking my head in disbelief.

January 28th, 2012

I must focus on the life and love that touched me, lifted me, and left lasting blessings in my heart. Tripp's life holds so much more meaning than the moment of death. When I find myself wrestling with the memories of a difficult, prolonged, or sudden and traumatic end, I try to shift my thoughts toward the light and the joy that Tripp's life brought to me. The love and life we shared will always outweigh the sorrow of loss.

After earning my certification in grief counseling, I began searching for a small space to open a grief center. My vision was to provide counseling and host meetups with other mothers in the area who had lost a child. Eventually, I found the perfect space.

I searched for the perfect décor that would create a warm, cozy atmosphere, with touches of hope and peace woven throughout.

Why Me? - Navigating the Unbearable Truth of Grief and Loss

February 7th, 2012

Along my journey, I met another mom who had also lost her son in a motorcycle accident, and we quickly became great friends. Deb, lovingly known as "Mamabang," played a big role in helping me set up my new grief center. Together, we worked tirelessly to prepare for its opening in just a couple of weeks.

After spending some time brainstorming, setting things up, and rearranging the furniture, we decided to call it a day and return the following day to put the clouds on the wall. When I got home, I received a message from Walt Hunter with CBS News in Philadelphia. They're going to do a story for the opening, which is especially meaningful as it also marks the second Angelversary of my son's passing.

The next morning, as I was on my way to pick up Deb, I mentioned that Walt Hunter from CBS News would be meeting us at the grief center to do a story on its opening. When I arrived at her house, she was laughing as she came outside, saying she had to quickly change after my phone call because she wasn't dressed for it—she had been in her camo! Walt and his camera crew arrived, interviewed us, and captured us putting the finishing touches on the wall. The story aired that evening at six and ten.

After all our efforts, we finally finished, and the space turned out beautiful—warm, welcoming, and inviting.

A special thank you to Deb Mamabang Schwartz for all her help. My brain was exhausted from all the brainstorming we did, but I couldn't have done it without her.

February 17th, 2012

It has been two years today since I last saw my precious son alive. I miss him with all my heart and soul. As life keeps moving forward, I will forever miss my sweet boy and everything he was and still is to me. I pray everyone has a good day. Mine has already begun with tears, so I returned back to bed for a little while longer.

I will never forget the first day my grief center opened. I was sitting at my desk, staring at Tripp's picture, thinking about him, especially since we had opened on his second Angelversary. Suddenly, I heard the door open. I scrambled to grab a tissue to dry my eyes, but it was too late. I could tell people had entered, and as I turned around, tears still streaming down my face, they asked, "Is this the grief center? We're looking for the grief counselor." Through my tears, I said, "Yes, that's me. Sorry, this is my son's second Angelversary, and I was just thinking about him." They were very sympathetic, and I soon realized they were reporters wanting an interview. I was so embarrassed, but everything ended up working out. After that, I did my best to keep it together.

Often, I would ask myself, *What were you thinking, Shirley?* I was still crying my eyes out, yet I believed I could help others who were grieving. And then I'd answer myself, *yes, I can, because it will help me too.* I wasn't giving up. I was going to do this.

The first client I ever had was a man who looked to be about 60 years old. His wife had made the appointment, and I scheduled him for the

Why Me? - Navigating the Unbearable Truth of Grief and Loss

next day since my schedule was wide open after just launching the grief center. He sat down, and we began with some small talk before transitioning into the session. I asked him how his son had passed, and he explained it had been five years since the accident. He also shared that he had been ordered by a judge to attend grief counseling.

Curious, I gently asked if he could share why. He sighed and said, "Yes. My wife and I were so deep in grief that we started growing marijuana in our basement. Smoking was the only thing that seemed to help us cope. I grew it under lights for three years. One evening, we had a friend over, and reluctantly, I took him to the basement to show him my crop. He asked me how I was managing my grief, so I showed him. He seemed fine with it—or so I thought."

The man paused for a moment, then continued, "The next morning, my wife and I were sitting at the kitchen table having our coffee when four police cars pulled up. They banged on the door, came inside, went straight to the basement, confiscated everything, and arrested me. Turns out, my 'friend' had reported us. Some friend, huh? And now, here I sit. I guess this is my punishment."

I felt so bad for him. He was required to attend eight weekly appointments. By the third week, he started bringing his wife with him, and they would talk about their son and share memories, though they avoided mentioning the betrayal they had endured. They were kind people, and I genuinely enjoyed listening to their stories.

That experience stuck with me. It was one of the first lessons I learned as I began hearing stories from parents who had lost their children and the unimaginable circumstances they often faced. Early in my grief journey after losing Tripp, I came to an important realization: **Do not judge others. No matter what. PERIOD.** Everyone grieves differently and processes loss in their own way. We are all just trying to survive the pain.

April 1st. 2012

This morning, I sat in church, crying as usual. It's something that happens every time I walk through the doors now. But today, the sermon touched me. In the Gospel of John, Chapter 9, where Jesus healed the blind man, I found something that struck me deeply. The Pharisees—well, they were a real piece of work, weren't they? In Verse 2, it says, "And the disciples asked Him, saying, 'Rabbi, who sinned, this man or his parents, that he should be born blind?'" Verse 3 says, "Jesus answered, 'It was neither that this man sinned nor his parents; but it was so that the works of God might be displayed in him.'"

The passage goes on to tell how Jesus spat on the ground, made mud, and rubbed it on the blind man's eyes, and after he washed them, he could see. It made me realize that a person can be physically healed, but if they have spiritual blindness, they won't see that they need healing.

Psalm 103 reminds us that our Lord is compassionate and gracious, slow to anger, and abounding in loving kindness. In Verse 14, it says that He knows us and is mindful that we are merely dust. I guess what I'm trying to say, though I can't quite explain it well, is this: count your blessings every day and keep your eyes on the Lord because He is our healing and our only way to find the joy that seems at times to be so far away.

What a journey we live. One day, everything is going smoothly, and the next, everything changes in an instant. It's like being forced onto the spinning wheel of grief, not knowing when it will toss us into an unfamiliar place. Finding the "new" us isn't easy. It's a long process, taking years. And all I know is that with each passing day, I miss my son, Tripp, more.

We have to feel to heal. We must allow ourselves to experience every moment of grief, and absorb it all. In time, you will understand why it's necessary. Every step, every tear, every second matters.

I highly recommend connecting with others who are on the same path. Find someone who is on the same journey, or someone further

Why Me? - Navigating the Unbearable Truth of Grief and Loss

along in their journeys—someone who can offer guidance and understanding. It can be one of the most healing tools. But be cautious because some people may bring you down and suck the life out of you. We all have to want to heal and move forward. If you find yourself surrounded by someone who is dragging you into negativity, walk away. Some people choose to stay stuck in their pain, and while that's okay, it's important not to let their darkness consume your healing process and keep you in a place that is hurting you and your healing, and it's not healthy.

We are different now. We've been changed, and we have to learn how to live without one of our children, or perhaps, our only child.

Grief is brutal, but we are not alone. Reach out when you need to. Others are walking the same path, and together, we can help each other heal.

We go through life living, not often thinking about death. Most of us experience the loss of grandparents or parents, usually after they've lived full lives, and we prepare for those moments, knowing they're coming. But losing a child? That's something we never imagine, never prepare for. When it happens, it's beyond our comprehension. We ask ourselves, *Why us? What did we do to deserve this?* The emotions that follow are overwhelming and frightening. The days and the months ahead seem like an endless, heavy fog filled with despair. We experience feelings we didn't even know existed.

People may tell us to "move on," "get over it," or "start living again," but the truth is, we can't. We're broken. Our hearts are shattered, and we struggle to pick up even the smallest pieces just to function. We often feel hopeless, like we've lost our direction, our purpose—and in many ways, we lose ourselves.

We have so many emotions inside, so many feelings that need to be expressed. *Emptying out*—sharing our grief—is healing. Without it, we continue to suffer. I urge all of you to reach out to another bereaved parent in person, someone who understands. You'll be surprised how much it can help to just talk. I've uncovered things from my past

I thought were resolved, only to find they weren't, and sharing those feelings with someone who's walked this path helped me heal.

Not everyone will be kind. Some people may judge, and they're the ones we need to avoid. But find the ones who are compassionate, who are kind, and lean on them. We're all in this together.

I remember those early days, the weeks, the months, and even the years, and it's not easy. It's an emotional rollercoaster. I pray for all of us that we find peace, understanding, and healing.

Oh, the expectations we place on others. By my third year on this journey, I realized that having expectations only leads to disappointment and pain. When we release those expectations, we free ourselves from the anger and frustration that come when others don't meet them. Letting go allows us to appreciate the kindness and thoughtfulness of others when they do something unexpected or say something meaningful. It feels so much more genuine and heartfelt when it comes without our anticipation or longing. At times we will have an expectation but will soon learn when it doesn't happen that we shouldn't have had it. I sure have learned my lesson, but it took me a while.

Below are a few of my expressions that I would post in my group:

-While we may never fully heal from the loss of our child(ren), we can strive each day to move forward. As we grow in our grief, we gain the ability to help others who are just beginning this painful journey. Yes, speaking with a newly bereaved parent can be incredibly difficult. It often pulls us back to places in our grief we thought we had left behind. But it also serves as a powerful reminder of how far we've come.

-In helping others, we see the progress we've made and recognize the gift of rediscovering joy. This doesn't mean forgetting or moving on; it means honoring the lives that meant so much to us while finding a way to live forward with love and purpose.

Why Me? - Navigating the Unbearable Truth of Grief and Loss

-When a piece of your heart is taken, the world becomes a shadowed, unforgiving place. It feels like a prison from which there's no escape. The cherished memories that once brought comfort now bring a hollow ache, leaving you feeling like an empty shell. Confusion clouds every thought, and the unrelenting pain consumes the love that once felt untouchable.

-We search desperately for meaning, only to confront the bitter truth—there is none. We are broken and shattered beyond recognition. The only solace comes from those who share the same unbearable loss. Scattered across the world, we find one another through our grief. This shared pain becomes a lifeline, connecting us in ways others cannot comprehend.

-Life becomes a spinning wheel, a chaotic cycle of hope and despair. We cling to the chance of better days, but when the wheel stops, we find ourselves in yet another unfamiliar, desolate place. Yet, we step on again, tentatively hoping for a gentler outcome, only to be thrown off, lost once more in the darkness. Despite the bruises, we keep rising, trying to piece ourselves together.

-Judgment from others adds to our burden, their cruel misunderstandings cutting deeper than words. Slowly, we realize that not everyone will care about or even acknowledge our pain. This realization deepens the grief—not just for our lost child but for the friends and family who have drifted away, unable or unwilling to walk this difficult path with us.

-Expectations only lead to heartbreak. Let them go. Embrace those who truly understand, for they become your lifeline. These friends, forged through shared sorrow, will never judge your brokenness. Instead, they will walk beside you, holding you up when the weight feels unbearable.

-The world keeps spinning, people come and go, and the grief persists. But one day, we will step onto that wheel, and when it finally stops, we'll find ourselves reunited with our child. In that moment, happiness and love will replace all the pain. The dark days of grief will fade, replaced by the pure joy of being together once more.

-Grief and love are forever intertwined; one cannot exist without the other. I have never hidden behind a mask or pretended to be okay when I am not. Don't be afraid to be who you are. We will never be the same person we were before, and that's okay. Embrace who you are becoming.

-Yes, we must work through our sadness. We cannot let it define us completely. But even as we grow into this new version of ourselves, we carry our children with us, keeping their memories alive in our hearts and minds.

-When the days are darkest, and it feels impossible to go on, remember this: you are your child's memory keeper. In living forward, you honor their life and ensure that their legacy endures. You are not alone. Together, we can carry both the weight of our grief and the light of their love.

-The spinning wheel begins to turn, hurling you into dark, colorless places where you feel lost and broken. Over time, the wheel slows, and we start to learn where to step off and how long to stay before we climb back on. But still, we miss our child(ren).

- "What do I do now?" That question resonates deeply because, in the wake of such loss, you truly don't know. Learning how to live again while feeling incomplete is one of the most heart-wrenching journeys imaginable.

-Grief is love turned inside out, and the deeper the love, the deeper the grief. Behind every smile, every moment of laughter, and every glimmer of joy, there's a shadow—a cloud of sadness that never truly fades.

-The spinning wheel has thrown me off into a place this time, and I'm wondering who I am. Almost ten years without my beautiful son And I am lost. Lost in a place trying to identify me. Who am I? I can't even grasp where I am. I question myself, but I have no answers. I know I am better because I no longer have that pain that once consumed me, but it's different now. A longing in my heart that just doesn't go away. Our souls are connected even in death. I have always believed everything happens for a reason, and I still do, but what is that reason? I won't know until it's over. I always pray for all of us, especially for the newly bereaved, because I know your pain, but also for those of us traveling this journey for many years, for the pain is still with us in a different way, somehow worse because the missing them is greater. God bless us all on this journey.

-TIME. It passes so fast. Sometimes so fast that we wonder where it has gone. In time, we forget, we re-live, we remember, we regret, we find love, we dream....and in an instant, everything can change in the blink of an eye. What does time do, then? TIME STOPS. Does time heal broken hearts? Does time heal wounds? My life has not been one of bliss and glory, neither has it been one of sadness or doom. I have fought and worked hard for everything. I have a wonderful awesome husband whom I know loves me with all his heart. I have two living children who I love so deeply and who mean the world to me. I have beautiful grandchildren. I drive a nice car and live in a nice home. I could go on and on, but it doesn't matter. A piece of me is missing, a huge piece, and all those wonderful things don't mean much anymore. Without my son......I am so broken... every day as I know, we all are. TIME?... I believe TIME helps because TIME takes away that excruciating pain we feel in the beginning. Now it turns into something else.... a yearning that can't be explained. Keep them close to your heart. Cry if you want to. Talk about them always. Cradle them in your heart always.

-Don't we all just sit at times and try to figure it all out? I know I do. The longer I am on this journey, the more I seem to understand or not understand. Grief is love turned inside out, but when I think about it, I conclude this: Grief is a much stronger emotion than Love. Yes, we love with all of our hearts, but after we lose a child, the grief becomes much stronger because we don't recognize how very much, we love. It makes sense to me. Grief really does become our friend over time because grief is what enables us to recall memories and smile because of the love we shared with our child no matter how long we had them. Grief changes us, and it doesn't have to be for the

Shirley Tripp Johnson

worse. Grief makes us real. Grief makes us see through different eyes. I was talking to someone the other day, and I mentioned the fact that her husband said he wanted the old her back. As true as that is for anyone's spouse, I replied with, when you are at one of our retreats, you are as close as you will ever get. No judgments. You can be who you are, expressing every emotion you have without anyone asking why. You can laugh, cry, sing, dance, fall on your knees in despair, or raise your hands, Praising God. It's whatever and whoever you are at the time. That's who we are. No masks. No faking. Just be. People who don't have support have a much harder time coming to a place of healing and although I don't think we will ever be healed in this lifetime, I do believe we can start the journey of healing, but only when we can be who we truly are and who we are because of our grief. We have to feel before we can heal. We have to talk about our loss over and over, and there will finally come a time when we won't feel that need so much anymore. We will NEVER forget our child who died...EVER. In the early years of grief, we have that need, and it's so very strong. We want to talk to anyone who will listen. Keep dancing with your grief....it will finally bring you peace within yourself. Grief really is your friend.

-As time goes on, I know I miss my son more and more. It has been 40 and a half months since I saw his beautiful face or received one of his special hugs. Tears are never far away as I go through my daily routine. They come without notice and, at times, for no apparent reason. Sometimes, I can smile through the tears and other times, I can't bring a smile to my face if I try. I look for him in everything. I have found that I feel him close to me in nature. We are here in a group that we never expected to be in. We come from all walks of life with different beliefs and lifestyles, and our children have died for so many reasons and causes here, but all the same, we are grieving the loss of a child or children. Our lives are forever changed, and we have to find our way down a path that leads us into the pit of hell at times, but then we are always given those glimpses of Heaven along the way. We are tossed to and fro like rag dolls, and our souls burn like an open wound that has salt poured into us, but as we travel this journey, that guy-wrenching pain begins to soften. Soften doesn't

Why Me? - Navigating the Unbearable Truth of Grief and Loss

mean we forget our child or let go of them. To me, it merely means learning to live with it so it starts to become who we are now. Someone we have to get to know who lives with a broken heart each and every day. I think I understand how difficult it is for other people to be around us after death because I know some times I can't stand to be around me either. Fun-loving and playful went somewhere after Tripp died. I think I still have it somewhere deep inside, and I am sure I will find it again somewhere along this journey, but first things first. If you can smile-smile, because that is joy. We can even find joy in the tears. If you are in the first year of your grief, don't expect too much from yourself because having expectations will only let you down, not just for yourself but for other people also. Live each day, try to find a little joy along the way, and just breathe. I believe that the first year is a conditioning of what is to come, and we all have to go through it to get to where we are going. We may not know where that is, but we will know when we get there. Hugs to all of you

-When loss comes into our lives, dreams are snatched away, and we are left wondering how to face the future. We feel like we've been thrown into a deep, dark hole with no way out. Loneliness becomes our only companion, and we lose all interest in the daily routine of life. The very things that used to occupy our time and bring us pleasure no longer have any significance at all.

-Grieving is hard work, and it takes lots of time to travel our journey of grief. There is no road map to follow, so we don't know when the next bend or twist in the road is coming. We can't tell where there are steep hills or flat terrain. When we seem to be traveling along okay, suddenly, we find that we've hit a mountain that seems almost like it's impossible to climb. Grief is new, unexplored territory.

-There is something amazing about our grief journey, though. It's hard to explain; yet it happens all of the time. A rainbow appears out of nowhere and gives us hope. A butterfly lights upon our windowsill, and we find ourselves smiling. A meal appears on our table from a neighbor and we suddenly feel less alone. An invitation

Shirley Tripp Johnson

to dinner comes, and we feel loved. The telephone rings, and we have a much-needed listening ear.

Just knowing that we have this added inner strength keeps us going until one day, we find that we are no longer in that lonely hole, but we are sitting among the flowers, and we can once again see beauty in life!

I am up at 2 am, which is not unusual. I always think about Tripp because usually, he would be up romancing a bowl of cereal with the dining room light on dim. He didn't like to be talked to when he was eating cereal and that was from a little boy on up to his adult years. I smile when I think of it now. That boy loved his cereal and went through about 10 boxes a week. Oh, how I miss buying cereal. I am 42 1/2 months into this journey, and I still feel so lost without him. He was my youngest child, and we were so. Close. One morning here, happy as can be, the next moment is gone. Killed by a negligent bus driver not paying attention. Ugh. I know he is never coming back, but I still feel, at times, this is a horrible nightmare, especially when I look up at the family photo with his big smile looking at me. I still feel sad, but I have accepted that he's not coming back. There are good days and some bad, but now I really try to honor my son through the way he lives. He was always happy and grateful for the day. He had such a positive attitude and I have learned so much through his death. For those of you just beginning this journey, you are blessed because you have found this group and people who understand. So many didn't have this and had to go it alone. I am grateful for all of you, and in the days and months ahead of you, you are going to begin to heal. Allow it to happen. You will never forget your child, but we must let go of the pain that holds us down in the darkness. After the first year, you should begin to feel a difference, for some at two years .... go with the flow.....you need to let go of the pain, but that doesn't mean letting go and forgetting your child. We can never do that.... just don't get so familiar with the pain that it keeps you in its grips........time really does heal ....I believe that now, I am in the healing process, but it doesn't mean I don't love my child and miss him; I am merely healing from the intense pain.

Why Me? - Navigating the Unbearable Truth of Grief and Loss

The year 2012 was a struggle, but I was slowly finding my way back, clawing my way out from the weight of brokenness that had been crushing me since Tripp was killed. I knew I was making progress. Though I stumbled often, I held onto the belief that as long as I kept moving forward, I would find my way.

In the beginning, I have to admit, I felt closest to Tripp when I was in my deepest suffering. I'm not entirely sure why, but I think I believed that the more I suffered, the more it proved how much I loved him. I was terrified of losing even a fraction of that love. Of course, I was wrong. It just felt that way.

As I began rediscovering moments of joy, little by little, I realized something profound—my love for Tripp didn't diminish. It grew. Tripp was such a happy soul, and over time, I came to understand that he wouldn't have wanted me to carry so much sadness. He loved life, and I knew he'd want me to continue loving mine.

For the past couple of years, I was really making an effort, and I have to give myself credit. I was pushing through the rubble, and finally starting to breathe again. I was feeling, I was healing, and I was learning to live forward.

Chapter 7
Rebuilding Through Brokenness

Let's talk honestly about grief.

Grief is the word we use to describe the entire experience of loss, but in many ways, it doesn't fully capture what we go through. Why? Because society has conditioned us to see grief as something negative and temporary—something to "get over."

But when a child dies, the grief lasts a lifetime. This is where the word falls short.

When we say we'll grieve forever, people often imagine the raw, early days of grief—

- Collapsing in tears,
- Struggling to get out of bed,
- Feeling withdrawn from life,
- Overwhelmed and unable to focus.

But long-term grief isn't always like that. Or at least, it doesn't have to be.

The problem is that we lack the right language to describe grief after those early, crushing stages. Having better words could help normalize what grief looks like as time goes on. I think the word would be best used as mourn. It would help others understand that talking about our loss isn't always about seeking sympathy, prayers, or sadness. Sometimes, it's simply a way to express love and honor the person who is no longer here.

"grief" versus "mourning." Can you explain the difference?

Grief is the constellation of internal thoughts and feelings we have when someone we love dies. Think of grief as the container. It holds your thoughts, feelings, and images of your experience when someone you love dies. In other words, grief is the internal meaning given to the experience of loss.

Mourning is when you take the grief you have on the inside and express it outside of yourself. Another way of defining mourning is "grief gone public" or "the outward expression of grief."

When families make the choice to not just grieve but also authentically mourn, they muster the courage and confidence to integrate the death into their ongoing lives. By authentic mourning, I mean openly and honestly expressing their thoughts and feelings from the inside to the outside – no pretense, no repression, no inhibitions. Somewhere in the collision between the heart, which searches for permanency and connection, and the brain, which acknowledges separation and loss, there is a need for all of us to mourn authentically.

What are the benefits of mourning?

Mourning is what makes it possible for us to experience, eventually, a sense of renewed meaning and purpose in our lives. The emotions we sometimes most want to avoid are the ones we most need to attend to. Authentic mourning is anchored in making the conscious choice to allow ourselves to mourn, to recognize that darkness sometimes precedes light, and to seek healing, repair, and transformation of our very being. And until we come to realize there is a natural, normal mourning experience that can result in meaningful transformation, we have little awareness of the need to experience the pain of grief.

Specific to the dead body, I often hear people say, "Well, it's just a shell." Of course, this is an attempt to render the body irrelevant and makes it disposable. Then the family can just focus on a "celebration" and make a swift, clean break from the loss. Yet, the more people try to "party" in the face of loss, the more they end up grieving and not mourning. These body-absent "parties" are often intentionally designed to merely skim the surface of our sadness – or ignore it altogether – and instead to focus on thinking happy thoughts.

Of course, I don't need to tell you that a dead body is not the same as the person we loved. No matter your spiritual beliefs, it is clear to anyone who spends any time at all with the dead body of someone they cared about that the soul no longer resides there. But when we are grieving – even those of us whose calling surrounds us with death and grief day in and day out – the mind seeks proof. So, if we are fortunate, we see the body, we touch the body, we spend time with the body... and our minds, which so very much want to deny the truth, cannot help but begin the process of acknowledging the reality of the death.

Dr. Alan Wolfelt, Center for Loss & Life Transition

Grief, at its core, is love. And there's nothing negative about love. ♥

It's okay to mourn for a lifetime because grief evolves. It changes and intertwines with life as the years pass, but it remains a reflection of the love we carry.

Embrace your grief as a testament to the love you've lost. It's proof that you lived it, that you loved deeply, and that you still love. And it's a reminder that even with grief, you can find a way to live again.

(Claire Bidwell Smith is an American therapist specializing in grief. George Bonanno, a professor of clinical psychology. Meghan Riordan Jarvis, a trauma therapist) All of these Authors have used certain phrases in their writings above.

One of the most difficult challenges during grief is finding meaning or making sense of your loss. The question, "Why me?" "Why did this have to happen?" is ultimately seeking some form of understanding.

As you work through this, here are some things to keep in mind:

Understand that finding meaning in loss is a deeply personal journey. Even after fifteen years, I have no clue, but I have learned to trust that God knows more than I do. While I wish my son were here, I find comfort in knowing he is safe in the arms of Jesus. What brings comfort to others may not be what works for you. While connecting with others who have experienced loss can offer valuable insights, don't be discouraged if their ways of coping or finding solace don't resonate with you.

Some of you may not be believers but know this: Our God loves you regardless. He loves you so much that He came to Earth and gave His only Son for all of us, so we could spend eternity with Him in Heaven. Remember that. Even if you don't believe, and no matter what you've done in this life, Jesus loves you, I promise.

It's easy to blame God, especially in the early days of grief. But as I look back on my life, I realize how many times He has saved me through struggles and challenges. While blaming Him might provide some temporary relief, I've found that He brings us through the pain slowly and at our own pace. I've learned that prayer has been a source of comfort for me—pouring out my heart and sharing my pain. And though it often feels like we're waiting, I believe that God gives us what we need when the time is right.

Look inward to your spirituality and beliefs. Everyone has a unique way of understanding the world, and that personal perspective is at the core of your spirituality. Reflect on how your faith and spiritual beliefs can help guide you in finding a sense of meaning that feels true to you.

As you progress on your grief journey, you will gradually begin to focus more on what you had and be grateful for the time you did have. You will always long for your loved one to return, but since that can't happen, you will carry them with you—in your heart and mind—forever, cherishing the joy and happiness they brought to your life. That never fades. They remain with you.

You will still have days filled with tears and sadness, but remember, no matter how many days, months, or years pass, it's all part of the grief process. I truly believe that this will continue until we take our last breath. Grief, over time, becomes something like a quiet companion. I know that may be hard to understand, especially after grief has dragged you through the darkest of times on your hardest days, but it's all part of preparing to become the new version of yourself.

Dealing with the "stuff of grief"—the possessions, clothes, and belongings of the person who has passed—can be incredibly difficult. Well-meaning friends may suggest that you clear everything out, while others may make requests, either subtly or not so subtly, for certain items.

The first thing to remember when handling the stuff of grief is that there are no set rules. You have the power to decide what to keep and what to give away. Just as with other aspects of grief, there is no right or wrong way to approach it, and there is no set timeline. You should only begin to sort through their things when it feels right for you when you are ready.

If you choose to keep any clothing, I suggest storing it in an airtight container, especially if it contains elastic, as it may deteriorate over time. I waited eleven years before going through my son's belongings while downsizing, and I can tell you it was incredibly difficult—even after all that time. It felt like losing him all over again. My daughter came over, and together, we began sorting through Tripp's belongings. One by one, we placed items into trash bags, hoping her boyfriend, Aseem, or her son, Landon, might be able to wear some of his clothes. It was anything but easy—it was utterly heartbreaking. Once she was gone, I sobbed uncontrollably, overwhelmed by the emotions.

That being said, everyone processes grief differently, and your experience may not be the same. However, based on what I went through, I would suggest going through items like clothing much sooner than I did. In hindsight, waiting so long made it even harder for me, and I believe it might have been a mistake to delay it for that long. But whatever works for you.

You don't have to act strong. Grief doesn't make you weak. What you learn is that it takes courage to navigate this journey. Courage is what helps you grow and reveals the person you're becoming. It takes big courage to walk the path of grief.

Build up your courage and allow yourself to release whatever you've been holding inside. Keeping your emotions locked away will only cause them to find another way to surface. Your emotions will come out in words, tears, or by talking about your child. I mentioned this earlier in the book. Address everything that comes up—it's all part of your rebuilding process.

I can honestly say that I am not the same person I once was. I am a better person now, and I continue to work on myself every day.

Remember to seek out joy, even in your mourning. It can be anything—a small moment that brings a slight smile to your lips. When you find it, hold onto it. In the beginning, joy may be fleeting, but as you practice finding it, those moments will begin to last a little longer.

I cherish the feeling of joy, though there are still times when a cloud of sadness seems to linger overhead—and that's okay. I find joy now, especially in the connections I've made and the time we share, which is a treasure to my heart.

I also find joy with my family, though it was very hard in the beginning because there was always a missing piece. At our gatherings, his absence is deeply felt, but we love him, we talk about him, and sometimes I even feel his presence. There are moments when I imagine him sitting beside me, and that thought brings me comfort.

Triggers will come, and I mean a lot of them. Be prepared—they can appear anywhere: in the grocery store, in your car listening to music, or even during a random commercial. Anything can spark a memory or a wave of emotion. You'll get to know your triggers quickly, but you can't avoid them—they're all around. The best you can do is go with it and let the moment pass.

There will also be things others say that may trigger you. I used to get so angry when someone would say, "What if you were hit by a bus today?" Since that's how my son was killed, I hated that phrase. I still hate it, though I've caught myself saying it on occasion. Be patient with others—they might not know about your loss or what may trigger you.

We have to work on ourselves, too. Even though we are broken and shattered, everyone else's life hasn't changed, and people often say thoughtless things. Every day, I take a moment to reflect and ask myself if I've reacted poorly or behaved in a way I could improve upon.

I want to acknowledge that it takes time to reach a place where you know you are healing—and you will get there, and you'll know when. That said, it's comforting to know that you can start working on things early in your grief if you feel ready. Looking back, I wish someone had knocked on my door and prepared me for everything I was about to go through when Tripp died. Maybe I would have found the strength to rise sooner.

Some days it's one moment at a time, one breath at a time. And if you find yourself falling into that black hole I mentioned earlier, that's okay too. Healing happens even in the depths of despair. Just don't allow yourself to stay there indefinitely. At some point, you must start looking up so you can climb back to the peak.

Fifteen years later, I still fall into that hole occasionally, but I don't stay there for long anymore. I've come to realize those moments are part of my healing process. However, it's important to remember that repeating the same routine day after day can trap you in a rut, and crawling out of it can be incredibly hard.

That's why I suggested earlier in the book to make a list and aim to do just a little more each day. If you can't, that's okay, but at least give it a try. Not right away, though. In the early days after your loss, you need that time to simply be—to feel the shock and numbness before beginning to move forward.

As time goes on, you might still find yourself struggling to get things done. That's why I strongly recommend making lists. Some days, I don't need one—but to be honest, most days, I do. My memory has gotten so unreliable that I'll think of something important one day, only to completely forget it the next.

To stay on top of things, I write everything down—even tasks I need to remember two days later. It's a simple habit, but it makes a big difference for me. If you've been having trouble keeping track of things like I do, it might be worth giving it a try. You never know—it could help you too.

As you begin to rebuild, each fragment starts to form a new shape—one that is unfamiliar to you and to those around you. But these pieces, scattered and jagged as they are, tell a story. They tell of your strength, your resilience, and your vulnerability. They reflect the loving and broken parts of you, creating a new version of who you are, and who you will become.

This version of you, though fractured, is whole in a way you never imagined. And through this journey, as painful as it is, you will find a new sense of self, one forged through love, loss, and the courage to rise again.

When we begin to rebuild from our brokenness, we often realize we need to retrain ourselves in certain ways. We're not the same person we once were. Habits change, our outlook on life shifts, and even the things we once enjoyed may no longer bring us joy.

Wherever your new path is leading, embrace the journey and adjust your sails as needed. If life is pulling you in a different direction, don't try to force your way back to how things used to be—that's not only difficult but unnecessary. It's not meant to be easy.

Your grief journey shapes the new version of you, and that's a gift. For me personally, I've come to like the person I've become through it all.

Let go of your expectations—it's one of the best things you can do for yourself. When you stop expecting, you protect yourself from disappointment and, in turn, lessen the sadness that can come when others don't follow through. I learned this lesson within the first six months after Tripp was killed, and it has been invaluable ever since. Now, I live without expectations. If something positive happens, I'm simply grateful.

I cannot stress enough how important it is to make connections with fellow grievers. When we lose someone, we need people to talk to—people who will listen without judgment. Take the time to get to know them. Friendships can form, even if it's difficult to find someone nearby. This is why online support groups are so crucial. Phone conversations are just as important. I truly believe that connection is the key to healing.

Take off the mask. Don't hide your feelings. If you're not expressing yourself, especially to your family, they won't understand when you fall into that dark place. Share how you're feeling every day, even though they may not fully understand. But they can learn that supporting you is the best way to love and help you. Your partner or children are suffering too because in many ways, they've lost you as well. Let them know how much you love them and that when you withdraw, it's not because you don't care. As you go through this grief, they will learn alongside you.

But please, make a promise to yourself—if you ever feel suicidal, reach out. Contact a suicide hotline or an online group and ask for help, or have someone call you or call someone. There's no shame in it. Many of us have had those thoughts, feeling like we couldn't go on, but reaching out for support is a step toward healing.

When we focus on our own growth, we become better equipped to support others starting their journey.

Chapter 8
Connecting with Fellow Grievers

Connections are incredibly important, and I cannot emphasize that enough. If anyone tells you that connecting with others who are grieving will only make you feel sadder, ignore them—that's simply not true. We need each other, and it's one of the best things we can do for ourselves and one another. The bond we share is stronger than anything else. Don't let anyone make you feel like your healing journey isn't valid or that you should heal in a way that doesn't feel right for you. It takes courage to heal, and without it, we can't find our strength, and so much of that strength comes from being around others who have lost a child too.

When I opened Wings of Hope Grief Center on February 17, 2012, the connections I had been yearning for truly began to form. Before the center opened, I had already met some incredible people who became friends, but after the center's doors were open, I was able to host meetings for grieving mothers. The space was warm and inviting, creating a safe environment where moms could begin to share their stories. At first, it was hard for many to open up, but over time, the stories flowed, and the tears were shed. We got to know each other in ways that words alone couldn't capture.

But the connections didn't end there. I also started a local grief group and began hosting gatherings at my home. The turnouts were always wonderful, and I'd prepare meals for everyone. Together, we would release balloons in memory of our children in my backyard. We lived in a two-story house with a walk-out basement, so I rented round tables and chairs, setting up a tarp to shield us from the sun or rain. On the upper level, I surrounded the chairs with beautiful pots of flowers. Some people brought drinks or desserts, but I always took care of the main meal. These mothers were incredibly special to me, and some would travel over two hours just to be there. Their

Why Me? - Navigating the Unbearable Truth of Grief and Loss

willingness to connect and share in such a profound way is something I'll always cherish.

In July of 2012, I asked my group, "My Child Has Wings," if anyone would be interested in having a conference in the Philadelphia area, and the response was overwhelming. I had attended a Compassionate Friends conference before, and I had always dreamed of starting my own. But I had a different vision for how I wanted it to look. I spent the next few months researching and planning, and just as I thought I was ready, my phone rang. It was a number from Virginia.

I hesitated before answering, but when I did, a woman named Renee introduced herself. She ran a support group for grievers and mentioned that her group was planning a weekend retreat in Gatlinburg, Tennessee, in the Smoky Mountains in November 2013 and asked me if my husband and I wanted to go. By this time, I had become fairly well-known in the grieving community. My grief was raw and outspoken, and somehow, a word about me had reached her. She shared the details, and I told her I would check with my husband, Dan, to see if he wanted to go, as the retreat was open to both single moms and couples. When Dan got home, I asked him, and his response was, "Whatever you want to do, Shirley. It's up to you."

So, I called Renee back and told her we would attend. She created a Facebook group for all the attendees and added me. Once I felt comfortable, I asked for pictures of everyone's child who had passed, as I wanted to surprise them with a video in memory of each child. I selected a song and found the perfect pictures to go with it, and then followed it with another beautiful song and a slideshow of all the children's pictures, and even included the shape of each state of all the people who were in attendance. It was a special moment, and everyone loved it. I was delighted.

There were many people at the retreat who came from all over the country, representing different states. At times, things felt a bit chaotic, as the planning hadn't been done as thoroughly as I would have liked. Despite the challenges, I learned a lot from the experience and still held on to my vision of what I wanted to create.

Most of the attendees were relatively new to their grief journey, with only a few having been on this path for a longer time. In the beginning, there was so much raw emotion and sobbing, as the early stages of grief can be incredibly intense. Despite the heaviness, many of those who attended chose to stay with us as we moved forward with our new vision, continuing the journey together.

I will never forget the day I stood at the front door of Mansion in the Sky and it opened to reveal Renee and Frank. I recognized Renee immediately—she had described herself to me as a large woman, and I had seen her photo on Facebook. Without hesitation, I walked up to her and said, "Hi, Renee, I'm Shirley." We embraced warmly, as though we'd known each other forever.

Just then, an older woman with long gray hair walked through the door. She had an almost ethereal presence, like an angel stepping into the room. She looked at me, her eyes soft yet piercing, and said, "Ahhh, you have an aura." I smiled and replied, "Thank you—I think."

Her name was Irma, a Native American woman and a minister. Over time, she became a close friend to many of us, attending numerous retreats and touching countless lives with her wisdom and kindness. She has been a profound inspiration to me and to everyone fortunate enough to meet her.

Irma was truly a blessing—a rare soul whose warmth and love light up every room she enters. She is a special lady, and I loved her with all my heart.

Why Me? - Navigating the Unbearable Truth of Grief and Loss

Irma attended several of our retreats, and her presence was nothing short of magical. We'd often find her outside, dancing in the rain, or gently anointing our heads with oil—a woman deeply connected to both spirit and nature.

She was a prayerful soul, always listening intently to others, offering comfort and wisdom. And oh, did she have stories—captivating ones that could hold your attention effortlessly.

Irma is in heaven now, reunited with her three sons who passed before her. But her memory lives on in the hearts of all who knew her. I will never forget the joy she brought and the light she carried whenever she was near.

Before we left Gatlinburg, Renee and I had a conversation and decided we could collaborate on a joint venture, but I made it clear that I had a different vision for how I wanted things to unfold. We agreed that I would fly to her house in Virginia, where we would work together to finalize the paperwork for submitting a 501(c)(3) charity. I already had some materials from my grief center, but we decided to rebrand the organization as Wings of Hope Living Forward Inc., Grieving Parents Healing Together.

Shirley Tripp Johnson

We made significant progress, and I was able to finish the remaining paperwork when I got back home. This was in mid-December of 2013, and it was the beginning of turning our visions into a reality.

After a lot of back and forth with LegalZoom's help to get all the paperwork edited to perfection and sent off for approval, Renee and I dove into planning, spending countless hours on the phone despite being in different states. Renee reached out to a contact she knew through her partner, Frank, who worked in the pool cleaning business and cleaned this guy's pool. Through that connection, we secured our first rental—a beautiful house on the ocean on Sandbridge Beach in Virginia—for May 2014. With our first retreat booked, we immediately began searching for another perfect location in Arkansas. We found a beautiful house near Greers Ferry Lake with breathtaking views of the lake and booked it for September 2014. The day before we left for this retreat, I received the IRS approval that we were an official 501(3)c charity.

The retreats were already thriving. We were building meaningful connections, helping others navigate their grief, and finding healing for ourselves as we shared weeks with these courageous, brokenhearted individuals.

At these retreats, all masks came off. We didn't have to pretend anymore. We could simply be ourselves, free from judgment. There was joy and laughter, and for once, we didn't have to worry about others misunderstanding or assuming we were "okay" again—because we weren't. Yes, there were plenty of tears and deep sadness, but it was all part of the healing.

The attendees left the retreats with renewed hope and new friendships that became like family—a "chosen family" bonded by shared experiences and understanding.

Joy is something we carry within us, no matter how small or hidden it may feel. At times, it might seem undeserved or impossible to reach, but when we do find it, it nourishes our souls. We must allow ourselves to embrace it, even if it's fleeting, because joy has the power to lighten the weight of grief and help carry us forward.

Why Me? - Navigating the Unbearable Truth of Grief and Loss

At every Wings of Hope Living Forward retreat, joy was something we always hoped to cultivate. Hope and healing came through sharing our personal stories, and in doing so, we gave others the courage to find their own. I've seen so many arrive at these retreats burdened by hopelessness and unable to feel joy. But by the end, they had discovered it—sometimes for the first time in a long while.

After returning home, people often shared how much they missed everyone. Spending a week together under one roof creates deep bonds. The retreats were carefully structured, which I loved. Without structure, things can easily unravel, but with it, the experience became purposeful and transformative.

There was so much planning that went into our retreats. There was always a beautiful video of our children that played at the beginning of the first night of the retreat. We would also plan our meetings, which took place every morning at ten o'clock. Additionally, we organized a gift exchange, a raffle, a craft project, a beautiful candle-lighting ceremony at the end of our week, and much more. Each candle featured a picture of our beautiful children, and we had a ceremony brochure to commemorate the event.

During our retreats on Sandbridge Beach, we would spend time painting wine bottles and filling them with small items, along with our names and numbers. Afterward, we'd take a boat ride and release the sealed bottles at sea in memory of our children, each corked with wax, into the sea. We'd always throw them in alongside a beautiful rose. Many times, a few bottles would wash up shortly after being released, so eventually, the captain began taking us out beyond the wake. One of the bottles I threw was discovered near the

102

Shirley Tripp Johnson

Bahamas by a Coast Guard officer while he was searching for a sunken ship. I received an email from his wife because she could read my email address through the bottle.

Here is the email message I received.

> Happy holidays!
>
> I would like to let you know that my husband, who is in the United States Coast Guard found the bottle that you sent out to sea in memory of Tripp. His boat was the first to respond to the missing ship, El Faro a couple months ago. He found the bottle in route, and put it right in his bunk for safe keeping throughout the remainder of the patrol. I would like to express my deepest condolences for you and your family's loss. I hope this gives you some comfort, especially over the holiday season.
>
> Happy holidays,
>
> Andrea Durando (and Dillon Durando currently on the USCGC Northland somewhere in the Pacific.

I wrote her back asking if she would send it back to me.

December 26th, 2015, I received it through the mail back to me beautifully wrapped in Christmas paper, with a warm note and a photo of the couple.

When we first started the retreats, I would come home feeling utterly drained and exhausted. I made an effort to stay strong for everyone who attended, but there were times when it was really difficult. Afterward, it would take me a couple of weeks to rebuild my strength.

Over the years, twenty-two retreats were held, and every single one was incredible. Many of us formed lasting friendships across the country—and even internationally—with those who attended. In the beginning, I wasn't sure how early in the grief journey someone should attend, but after hosting these retreats, I came to believe that the earlier, the better.

Why Me? - Navigating the Unbearable Truth of Grief and Loss

Yes, it was difficult. It's intimidating to travel somewhere new and spend a week with total strangers, especially when you're in a state of deep brokenness. But I witnessed people as early as three months into their grief rise from the ashes and go on to create their charities to help others. It's not for everyone, but for those who feel the passion, it can be transformative.

I feel so blessed. Through the retreats, I've had the privilege of meeting some of the most incredible people, and I treasure every one of them. Age doesn't matter—young or old, the bonds we form last well beyond the retreats. While I would give anything to have Tripp back, I am deeply grateful for the beautiful souls I've encountered on this journey. Together, we've shared tears, laughter, and everything in between, finding healing in each other's presence.

There's a unique and unbreakable bond among those who have lost a child. It's a connection rooted in understanding, free from judgment, and full of love. We've become a family—a family that stays with you forever.

I can't stress enough how deeply I believe in the power of connections. Yes, you can have friends, and yes, they can listen, but no one—no one—can truly understand the depth of the loss of a child unless they've lived through it themselves. No one.

The beauty of these connections is that you can cry together, sit in silence, or simply be there for each other, knowing that they are always just a phone call away, day or night. As I sit here now, I think about all the times I reached out to broken, shattered people, only to later learn they were on the brink of suicide, but my phone call gave them just enough hope to keep going. It breaks my heart to know that some of us have felt so desperate, including me, but there is no shame in that. We are still standing, and we will keep moving forward.

The retreats were truly wonderful. As the years went by, the retreats began to consist mostly of familiar faces who already knew each other well, with a few new participants each time. This dynamic only made things better. When a newbie came in, they could see the close

Shirley Tripp Johnson

bond between those of us who had attended before, and it made them feel more comfortable as they arrived.

There are a few of us who have remained extremely close, even now and I am so incredibly blessed for their friendships.

Through grief counseling and organizing these retreats, even though I was shattered and broken in the beginning, I was healing alongside the people I was trying to help. Telling my story over and over, listening to others, pouring out my heart, and discussing things I never thought I would talk about, helped me more than I could have imagined. By emptying myself, I knew I had begun to heal. I am so grateful that I didn't end my life because witnessing others heal and rediscover joy has been such a blessing to me. Every time those dark thoughts crossed my mind, I thought of my kids, and they truly saved me without even knowing it. I thank God every day for guiding me through this journey of grief. Though I'll carry it with me for the rest of my life, I've found joy. I've made so many new friends, and for that, I am deeply grateful.

I wish I could include all the beautiful photos from the retreats and gatherings in this book, but there are so many, and some people may prefer not to have their pictures shared. So, I won't include them. However, I carry with me countless wonderful memories from those years. With each gathering, I healed just a little more. Being around other moms, in particular, was such a vital part of my healing. I can't fully explain the joy and camaraderie we shared, and we had so much fun together.

I hope that one day someone will feel inspired to organize retreats again, bringing the grieving together for a week-long stay. These retreats are true nourishment for the soul. Although we no longer host them, I deeply treasure the time I still get to spend with some of the incredible women I've grown close to over the years.

The friendships and bonds formed through these retreats are priceless, and I thank God for blessing me with the opportunity to share this journey with Renee for so many years. It was a privilege and a joy to be part of something so meaningful.

Why Me? - Navigating the Unbearable Truth of Grief and Loss

It's been fifteen years; I still cry every day because I miss Tripp. With each tear, I'm still healing. Sometimes, I get thrown back to a place I don't wish to visit, but I've learned to accept that it's part of the process. Now, I just go with it. And if it gets too overwhelming, I can always reach out to one of my grieving moms. Talking it out, pouring it all out, always helps. It brings me comfort and reminds me that I'm not alone on this journey. Remember to connect. Connect. Connect.

In the next chapter, I want to share more of my reflections from my third year of grief and beyond—not to make you think things don't get better, but to help you understand the journey. Even as I knew I was healing, there were still days and nights that felt as raw as if I were new to my grief. Yet, it was different. The unbearable pain had begun to ease. It still hurt—and it still does today—but I had learned to carry it with me.

We just have to keep moving forward, bringing our grief along as a part of us, and eventually, we begin to find comfort in it. Remember, grief is simply love turned inside out.

Chapter 9
Random Thoughts and Emotions through the years

I'd like to share a few more reflections on my journey. The dated entries below come directly from my journal. Writing these thoughts down allowed me to look back and see just how far I'd come. It also helped me navigate the uncertain path ahead. My thoughts were often scattered, and at times, I couldn't piece them together—and that was perfectly okay.

August 3, 2012

Today, remember your son or daughter with a big smile! Don't let any negative thoughts come your way, and if one tries to slip in, immediately stop it and replace it with a precious memory of your child. There still might be tears but when we can get to the point where we can smile and tear, it's progress. Finding joy through the pain, living forward. Can we all vow together and do this?

August 1, 2013

I must be a nut. I was watching TV tonight, and a song was on, and I came out of the bathroom dancing....looking at my fat self in the mirror, and even though I was having fun, I thought, OMG, you look like an idiot. I call it sappy and had. I can be very happy and all of a sudden get very sad or just the opposite and be very sad and get really happy. It is a roller coaster of emotions. Trying to find joy in the moment only for it to turn to tears. We have to try and catch that joy when we can no matter what. I imagine now the times Tripp and I would cut loose and dance together. Believe me, neither of us was a dancer, but just thinking about our joy makes me smile even though it makes me cry. Do any of you feel this way at times?

August 25th, 2013

Joy is found in the little things, like when your lips curl up into a smile. It could be a butterfly fluttering by, a bird singing, a baby's innocent giggle, or even something funny on TV. Hold on to those moments, no matter how small. We have to seek out our joy again.

Don't expect it to just appear after losing a child—it won't. But joy is everywhere, and it's within all of us. It's okay to find joy, to be joyful, to laugh, and to have fun. We are still here, still alive, which is something to celebrate.

Live fully and make our children proud. This is how we keep their memories alive—by embracing our joy again because that's what they were to us: our joy. Forever and always.

February 26, 2014

Sometimes, I still can't wrap my mind around the fact that my baby boy, Tripp, is gone. This morning, I woke up thinking about his accident, wondering if he felt anything in those final moments. I was told he died on impact, and I desperately hope that's true. But sometimes, I can't help but question if they just tell us that to ease our pain. The thought of him suffering would shatter my heart even more.

Then I think about those of you who were there when your child passed, and my heart aches for you. There are so many different circumstances, yet we're all in the same boat—missing our children and wishing with everything we have that we could have them back.

Four years into this journey, the gut-wrenching pain has lessened, but the ache of missing him only grows stronger with each passing day. I miss everything about Tripp. I even miss the little things I used to find frustrating—like his messiness. I'd give anything to have it all back, and I'd never say a word about it. I know many of you understand exactly what I mean.

Sometimes, I think I catch a glimpse of him, but when I look closer, no one is there. Could it be him? I don't know. Tripp taught me so

Shirley Tripp Johnson

much during his time here—he truly had an old soul. I wish I were more like him. He lived every day to the fullest, embracing life with an energy and spirit that inspired everyone around him.

On his angelversary, his best friend emailed me, saying Tripp would want me to "live it up." He told me that Tripp loved me dearly and would want me to do the things we used to do together—or even try new things I imagined sharing with him. I know in my heart that's true. Tripp would want me to live, even though it's so hard without him.

I miss him more than words can express. Even though it's been four years, the longing for him only deepens. Tripp was an inspiration, not just to me but to everyone who knew him. He was my youngest child and my greatest teacher.

I miss you, Tripp. I'll never forget you, and I'll always treasure the beautiful memories we shared.

January 26th, 2015

Wonderful memories in this family photo.

On February 17, my baby will be gone from this earth for five years. I honestly don't know where the time went, but I know that the way I feel now has no comparison to the way I felt in the years leading up to now. "Time" truly is a healer. "Time" doesn't take away from us

Why Me? - Navigating the Unbearable Truth of Grief and Loss

our memories and the love we shared with our child(ren). "Time" has taken away that gut-wrenching, all-consuming pain that I felt 24/7 in the beginning, but what remains is the intense feelings of the Love I have for Tripp and my longing to just have him here with me. I miss him with everything I have. I knew early on (13 months) that I had fallen into a dark place that I could not stay in, and it had become familiar to me. I felt closer to Tripp in that dark place. I was afraid of any kind of light. I didn't know what to do except pray. I also knew that God helps those who help themselves. It was a struggle and still is, but I give what I have every day to help myself live forward. Some days suck big time because I fail miserably, but I have many more good days now.

Almost five years now, and at times, I take time to really reflect since Tripp was killed.

My heart aches for all of you. We are all in our "OWN" place in Grief. Wherever you are in Grief and if you are struggling:

Know there is hope in the days ahead.

Time is a healer. I believe this.

If time isn't helping, get to know the Lord.

Letting go doesn't mean "letting go" of your child, only the pain.

Think of memories that make you smile even if you are crying.

Look at pictures and cry your eyes out.

Cry every day.

Be compassionate. Overlook your feelings if need be and do the right thing.

Understand that everyone is different. Don't insult people because they don't think the same way as you.

Meet other grieving parents. (Essential)

Talk about your child every day, even if you're talking to yourself.

Wear expressions of your grief. (People do ask questions)

"Never" expect anything from anyone. Having Expectations only hurt "You".

If something good happens- Great!

Do not pretend your child is not DEAD. He/She is dead. That is DENIAL.

Feel sorry for yourself and have a pity-party -JUST don't invite anyone else. Do this every day. (Really, yes) I do, and it helps me.

Do what makes "YOU" happy now. You are sculpting your "NEW NORMAL".

October 3rd, 2015

When a part of you is taken, the world becomes a dark place, a place where we fight like hell to get out of, but there is no escape. Our precious memories are invaded, leaving us an empty shell. Confusion surrounds our every thought, and finally, we lose ourselves in the love that once was untarnished. We search for meaning, but no matter how hard we try, there is none. We are broken and shattered beyond repair, and the only people who understand our pain are those who have endured the same. We are scattered all over this world, but our grief brings us together. We jump on that spinning wheel and hope for the best, always struggling to have better days, but when it finally stops, we are at a new destination, only to be lost once more. We cautiously step onto the spinning wheel again, hoping for a better outcome, but we are always thrown off into a different place that is confusing and dark. Shattered and broken, we keep getting up, trying to pull ourselves together as others judge us so cruelly. We go through our new life wondering if anyone even cares about our sadness. They don't. It doesn't take long to realize this and it only makes our sadness worse, now grieving for the friends and family who once were there for us but now have turned their backs because they say we are to broken. We mustn't have any expectations of other people. We are the ones who get hurt. Embrace the people who do understand because they become your new friends and will always understand your grief. This ole' world keeps spinning, and people will leave us, but one day, we will jump on the spinning wheel, and when we are gently tossed off, we will be with our child again, happy and smiling. We won't remember all those bad days we had when we were on the spinning wheel. Grief and love go hand in hand. We can't have one without the other. My son Tripp has been gone from this earth for five years, seven months, and sixteen days and I cry every day. I miss him with all my heart. I have never worn a mask or pretended to be okay when I am not. Don't be afraid to be who you are. We will never be the same person that we were before so just embrace the person you are now and go with it. Yes, we have to work on ourselves and our sadness. We can't allow that to overcome the person that is unfolding. We will never stop missing or loving our children no matter what, but we can embrace the loss, hold them in our hearts, and live forward, always keeping their memories alive and especially alive in our hearts and minds. Just know you are not alone and when times are rough and you feel you can't go on, just remember, you are your child's memory keeper.

February 16th, 2016

Don't we all have those moments when we just sit and try to figure it all out? I know I do. The longer I walk this journey, the more I seem to understand or, at times, not understand. Grief is love turned inside out, but when I think about it, I've come to this conclusion: Grief is a much stronger emotion than love. Yes, we love with all our hearts, but after we lose a child, grief becomes more powerful because we don't fully realize how deeply we love until they are gone. To me, that makes sense.

Grief becomes our companion over time because it's through grief that we recall memories, smile at the love we shared with our child, no matter how long we had them. Grief changes us, but it doesn't have to change us for the worse. It makes us real. Grief opens our eyes and helps us see the world differently.

I was talking to someone the other day, and she mentioned her husband wanted the "old her" back. As true as that might be for any spouse, I replied, "When you're at one of our retreats, you are as close as you'll ever get to being the old you." There are no judgments. You can be who you are, expressing every emotion without anyone asking why. You can laugh, cry, sing, dance, fall to your knees in despair, or raise your hands in praise. Whatever you are in that moment, that's who you are. No masks. No faking. Just be.

For those without support, healing can be much harder to find. I don't believe we will ever fully heal in this lifetime, but I do believe we can start the journey of healing. That can only happen when we allow ourselves to be who we truly are, shaped by our grief. We have to feel before we can heal. We need to talk about our loss, again and again, until one day, the need to speak about it isn't as strong. I truly believe that. But one thing is certain: We will NEVER forget our child. EVER.

In the early years of grief, that need to talk is overwhelming. We want to tell anyone who will listen. Keep dancing with your grief. It will bring you peace within yourself. Grief does become your friend.

November 21st, 2016

Time. It passes so quickly, sometimes so fast, that we find ourselves wondering where it has gone. Over time, we forget, we relive, we remember, we regret, we find love, we dream... and in an instant, everything can change in the blink of an eye. So, what happens then? Time stops.

Does time heal broken hearts? Does time heal wounds? My life hasn't been one of endless happiness or despair—it's been a mix of both. I've fought for everything I have. I'm blessed with a wonderful husband who loves me with all his heart. I have two children who mean the world to me, and beautiful grandchildren. I drive a nice car and live in a comfortable home. I could list all the good things, but in the end, they don't matter.

There's a piece of me missing, a huge part of my heart that will never be whole again. Without my son, I am broken... every day, just as many of us are.

Time? I believe time does help. Time eases the excruciating pain we feel in the beginning, but as time goes on, the pain turns into something else... a longing, a yearning that words can't explain. Keep them close in your heart. Cry when you need to. Talk about them always. Cradle them in your heart, always.

January 26, 2017

Those who know me understand that I'm never shy about expressing my opinion. I don't claim to always be right, but I know I'm not always wrong either. Tonight, I read something that upset me. I come across things like this often, but this particular one hit home. I'm a Christian and a spiritual person, but I will never stand on a self-righteous pedestal and talk down to others like I saw tonight.

After the loss of a child, many of us get angry with God for taking them away. I did, too, but only briefly because I came to realize that life is just unpredictable. Accidents, illness, violence, mental health issues, and so much more happen, and we need to accept that. God doesn't cause these things, but in our grief, we often want to place blame on someone. And that's understandable.

What bothers me, though, is when people push the idea that "all you need is Jesus" and that he will take away your grief and sorrow. That is simply NOT TRUE. Grief is not something God will just take away—grief is love turned inside out, and God would never take away our love because HE IS LOVE. Grieving after a loss is not a failure. It's part of the healing process, and we all go through it.

Those who try to deny their grief, thinking that God will just remove it, are, in my opinion, in deep denial. I've seen it happen—people who didn't allow themselves to grieve, and then, eventually, their grief caught up with them, coming back stronger than ever. Denial doesn't help—it only makes things worse.

The bottom line is this: Grieve. Grieve in your own way. Don't let anyone dictate how you should grieve. People will be critical—family, friends, even strangers. But so, what? It's not their loss; it's yours. Yes, we eventually heal and grow throughout this journey, but the loss of a child is something we don't just get over. Not anytime soon, and certainly not by someone telling us to "just move on."

Stand your ground. Be honest about your feelings, and if people don't understand, that's their issue, not yours. If you stay silent, they will never know what you're going through. Speak your truth. If they can't handle it, walk away.

Now, as for this idea that "God will take away your grief"—that's simply wrong. The people who say that have never lost a child, and I believe their perspective would change drastically if they did. I pray they never have to experience that kind of pain.

My advice is this: Don't get stuck. What we do repeatedly becomes a habit. Habits become comfortable, even though they're hard to break. Grief is no different. It can become a habit, too. But eventually, we realize what we're doing and work to overcome it. We'll never get over losing a child, but we can begin to heal, bit by bit.

I'm almost seven years into this journey, and some days are good, and some are tough. I still cry every day because I miss my son. I can't just push him out of my mind, and neither can any of you. In this group, we all share a common bond—our love for our children. Whether we've lost them recently or many years ago, the love and the longing are the same. We are broken, but we are also resilient.

February 17th, 2017

So many people think they've had bad days, but I've had a front-row seat to the most heartbreaking and devastating days of my life. On February 17th, 2010, at 7:26 am, my youngest son took his last breath on this earth. That day, my world shattered, and everything I knew about life changed forever.

I thank God every day for my children, Jeremiah and Deidre, my husband Dan, and the few close friends who stayed with me through my darkest days. The old cliché that time heals all wounds? It's simply not true. Time doesn't heal; it only intensifies the sadness of missing a child you loved with every part of your being. Grief is love turned inside out, and the more you love, the more you grieve.

I've found myself in some incredibly dark places over the years, but through it all, I've managed to rise again, and find joy, only to fall back into the valley of grief. I used to struggle with this cycle, but now I understand it. The darkness is where I find my strength to keep moving forward. It's a hard concept for some to understand, but know this: you can't fix it. You can only sit and listen. If you can't even do that, then there's not much else to offer.

Tonight, I sit and think. The last phone calls I've had with my family were made by me. No one calls me anymore, possibly because they don't want to hear about Tripp. I ask myself—what if you had to choose which child to lose? Would anyone want to hear about that child's life, or would they shy away from it? That's how it feels. It happens to all of us, and it's a sad reality.

Through this journey, I've made so many wonderful friends who, like me, have lost children. I love them all, and I would give every one of them back if it meant I could have Tripp again. Six years have passed, and it still feels like just yesterday.

I don't understand why, but I know that someday I will. And when I do, it probably won't even matter anymore. But for today, the questions remain. I'm human, and my heart is broken. I know it won't truly heal until I see Tripp again in heaven.

I just wish more people would show empathy for the brokenhearted—not to fix us, but to simply listen. That's where the healing lies. We need to talk about our loss, over and over, because our children matter. They existed. Tripp existed. He lived, and he will always live in my heart.

TrippNAintez 10-5-82 – 2-17-10. I will miss you forever.

March 27, 2017

Tonight, I sit here with a heart so full it brings me to tears. I've tried to go to bed, but the emotions won't let me sleep—so here I am, awake again. My tears are both happy and sad, a mix of emotions that feels strange but is undeniably real. I'm heartbroken as I miss my son, yet deeply grateful for the incredible friendships I've made on this journey through grief.

If I could have Tripp back, I'd trade it all in an instant. But since that's not possible, I find myself blessed to have this extended family of friends who understand. I know I talk about the retreats often, but they truly mean the world to me. They give me hope and renewal, the kind of support I need again and again on this path. These gatherings are more than just events—they're a lifeline, a reminder that we are not alone. We've built a family, and together we've found a way to "Live Forward."

Each of us has our own story and our unique definition of grief. But when we're together, there's no need for masks or pretense. It's raw, it's real, and it's healing. We learn so much from each other. I'm especially excited about the next retreat in May—our group will include a mom flying from Great Britain, as well as friends from California and other states. We'll share memories of our children, laugh, cry, and create meaningful experiences together.

Eight years ago, I never could have imagined this for myself. Back then, I had all my children, and life felt perfect. One second changed everything. Now, I'm grateful for this community, for those who have stayed in this group and reached out to others, especially those who are new to this journey. My heart aches for the ones just beginning, feeling helpless, confused, and overwhelmed. Believe me, we've all felt that way.

Tonight, seven years into this journey, I find myself tearful again. I miss Tripp so much. He was my baby, even at 27, and he was proud to be a mama's boy. Nothing can fill the void he left in my heart. Grief is relentless—it truly sucks. But I try to remind myself to be thankful that he was mine, even if only for a short time. That thought isn't always comforting, but it's something I hold onto.

Seven years later, the tears still come. Tonight, they're flowing freely. I just miss him so much. He was such a joy, such a light in my life. And I will carry that light with me always.

May 1st, 2017

So many people tell us to move on. But how can we? We carried our children, we gave birth to them, and they became a part of us. That connection doesn't fade, no matter how much time has passed. Grief is love turned inside out—the deeper the love, the greater the grief.

As the years go on, it changes. We don't stop missing them; if anything, we miss them more as time moves forward. The unbearable pain of the early days may ease, but something else takes its place. And I think it's even harder—it's the reality of it all finally setting in.

Seven years later, the day he died still feels like yesterday. Time has passed, but it's different now. The numbness and shock are gone, and what's left is the painful reality: he's gone. I miss him so much.

June 18th, 2017

Tripp was my baby, and I still can't believe he's not here. It's been seven years and four months, and my life has been changed forever. No matter how hard I try, Tripp remains at the forefront of my mind, always accompanied by an ocean of tears. That suffocating pain in my heart has shifted over time, but what I feel now seems even harder in a different way. Missing my baby boy is just too much at times.

Today, I went to gymnastics meet where my granddaughters were performing, and it was wonderful. My thoughts and presence were entirely for them. But as soon as I got home, everything changed. Tripp flooded my memory once again. I've grown accustomed to these moments, but they're still overwhelming.

I know I'll never truly get over losing my baby, but I long for some sense of normalcy—even though I'm not sure what that looks like anymore. I'm certain many of you understand that feeling. It's like a cloud of sadness that follows us around.

But maybe we can reframe it. Instead of a sad cloud, I'm starting to think of it as a grateful cloud. Because Tripp was mine—he was in my life for 27 wonderful years. (Easier said than done, I know.)

Sending hugs to all of you. I'm so grateful you're here. Knowing I'm not alone and that we have each other to walk this journey with makes such a difference. I'm thankful for our retreats; I'm not sure how I'd manage without them. Missing my son today and every day. He was truly a blessing.

Shirley Tripp Johnson

August 7th. 2017

I was born and raised in Arkansas where I resided for forty years then met my wonderful husband Dan and we moved to Michigan, now living in Pennsylvania. When I Lived in Arkansas, I met a gal named Joyce and we become best friends and through all these years, she has always been there for me. She has never had any children of her own but knew mine well. She ended up marrying a man from Pennsylvania and lived here for several years. Anyway, her mother-in-law passed away recently and the funeral was today. Last night I had such high anxiety about attending that funeral today. I didn't get to sleep until four am this morning and I had to be at the visitation at nine. I woke up shaking with high anxiety and tried so hard to talk myself out of going. The weather was bad but I got up, showered and headed over on my hour and a half drive. When I arrived at the church, I was a mess, shaking. When I walked in and walked toward her, she looked at me with questioning eyes? She said to me, what is wrong. I told her I was experiencing high anxiety and I just needed to sit down so I went inside the church. She came in later to ask me to sit with her and her husband during the funeral and I Told her no. I communicated to her there was no way I could sit in front of that casket but I appreciated her asking and she understood. As they brought the casket in, the family followed. As Joyce walked by me, sitting in the back pew, she handed me a box of Kleenex. I smiled when she threw them in my lap as I had told her the story about people giving us only one Kleenex when we are crying and how it becomes a wadded up little snotty piece of falling apart tissue as we try and use it over and over again with snot and tears Dripping from it and it is shredding into little pieces. She remembered. I guess what I am saying is this, cherish those friends who really listen and understand. I drove home in the pouring rain and I could barely see, hydroplaning all the way home. I was totally wasted by the time I got home. Fell to the couch and went to sleep. When I was at the church, I looked up and saw the most beautiful thing I had ever saw. It was Jesus hanging on the cross and I began to cry. I thought about his mother and pain and agony she must have felt as he hung there after he was tortured brutally. All I can say, is that I am grateful through all the anxiety I experienced. God is good and I know I will see my son again. God bless us all.

September 14th, 2019

I couldn't help but laugh as I recalled this memory tonight. Tripp called me and was so very sick, and I, as a mother, felt so helpless. I told him he needed to get in to see a doctor and he said he was going to Dr. Tanner the next day. Silence fell upon me as I choked a little and asked, isn't he the Veterinarian? Yeah, he answered; he doesn't charge me anything. I can only imagine him sitting in the vet's office waiting room and getting called back with no pet. His best friend's dad was a Vet, and he could always depend on him for medicine. It makes me chuckle every time I think of this as tears roll from my eyes. I miss my boy and all the crazy, but I love the memories. I just wish he was here to tell me not to sweat the small stuff, and it's all small stuff.

October 27, 2019

The spinning wheel... it's thrown me into a place I didn't expect, and now I'm left wondering who I really am. Almost ten years without my beautiful son, and I feel lost. Lost in a space where I'm trying to figure out who I am now. Who am I? I can't even seem to grasp where I am in life. I question myself, but the answers are elusive.

I know I'm better in some ways—I no longer feel consumed by that all-encompassing pain—but it's different now. There's a longing in my heart that won't go away. I truly believe our souls remain connected, even in death. I've always believed everything happens for a reason, and I still do, but what is that reason? I don't think I'll know until it's all over.

I always pray for all of us—the newly bereaved, because I know your pain all too well. But I also pray for those of us who have been walking this journey for many years, because the pain is still with us, just in a different way. Somehow, it feels worse because the missing them has grown greater with time.

Shirley Tripp Johnson

God bless us all as we continue on this journey.

> What moves through us is a silence, a quiet sadness, a longing for one more day, one more word, one more touch, we may not understand why you left this earth so soon, or why you left before we were ready to say goodbye, but little by little, we begin to remember not just that you died, but that you lived. And that your life gave us memories too beautiful to forget.
>
> Author Unknown

February 17th, 2020

On February 17th, 2010, my life changed forever when my youngest son, Tripp, was tragically killed at twenty-seven years old. Ten years have passed since I saw his beautiful face or felt his tight hugs. It's a nightmare that is impossible to wake up from. Nothing can prepare us for such a loss. It leaves a path of devastation with emotions so intense there is no escaping them. I have been in the valley (dark hole) more times than I can count, where the darkness is indescribable and cruel. At times, early on, I thought I would never emerge and see light again. I quickly learned that the "hole" was where the healing was taking place, and I just had to go with it. It's such a lonely place, a place where you feel everything and nothing. A place that drags your heart over jagged edges and rips your soul apart, leaving you broke and bleeding, and you feel as though no one even cares. Your heart aches so bad that you want to rip it out. About the time you think you're never coming back, you see the light peeking out from behind your cloud of emotions, and you slowly find yourself standing back on the peak, finding joy and smiling while thinking about the precious memories. The holes are further in-between now but they do still exist. I have had to allow myself to feel all of my emotions and acknowledge the hole that exists and that it cannot be filled up with anything or anyone else. It's just empty, holding on to all of my precious memories when my family was whole. Grief is love turned inside out. Where there is great love, there will be great grief.

Why Me? - Navigating the Unbearable Truth of Grief and Loss

I miss Tripp so much that, at times, I feel as though I can't breathe. Tears fall when I least expect them every single day. Time has flown by so fast, but I can still remember that horrific day like it was yesterday.

What I describe below were the worst days of my life so if you know someone who has lost a child, be gentle when they begin their journey and even years later. It is devastating! It is haunting! It is lonely. ......and remember, if you can't imagine it, we certainly can't explain it.

Written several years ago: After Tripp was killed, I learned the true meaning of despair. My heart was shattered into a million little pieces, leaving an empty shell inside me. Cries of disbelief shouted from my hollow heart and the pain I suddenly felt was like a ragged knife cutting through my soul. I was so broken, my world stopped, I was so shattered that when I fell to my knees screaming, I didn't want to get up. I felt dead inside and I didn't know how I was even breathing. I stood in absolute darkness and I knew, deep in my heart and spirit that I was never going to get better. My child was dead and he wasn't coming back. The road I was on was surely going to end in tragedy..............but it didn't. I did not think I would make it through. My days consisted of, how could I go on when I was suffocating inside, consumed with endless tears and pain as I paced aimlessly from room to room searching for something, anything to make me feel better... I would cry out WHY? Why, my boy. God help me. I was so angry. How could this even be true? Lord help me...Do you even hear me??? I knew I was going to lose my mind. I couldn't focus, I could barely function. I kept my nose buried in Tripp's clothes several times a day as I wept hopelessly. My heart became a piece of stone. Vivid memories would rush my mind and heart coupled with a sense of disbelief and panic, swelling into an overwhelming feeling that I just couldn't go on. Those feelings were often difficult because I tried so hard to avoid everyone. In my heart I knew I had to go on, I just couldn't figure out how. The pain was so intense. I just wanted to feel normal again, but what I wanted was to have my son back.

Shirley Tripp Johnson

Now, ten years later after my heart was shattered into a million broken pieces, I am surviving and continuing to live forward. It's rough and it hasn't been easy. I am so grateful that I have my two wonderful children, Jeremiah and Deidre, my grandchildren and my husband who have been understanding and put up with me when I didn't want to even be inside myself. Thank you. I love you all very much.

We love you to Heaven and back Tripp Taylor and miss you so much. Our hearts are broken without you. 10/5/82 – 02/17/10

February 17th, 2021

Here I am again, eleven years later. The day my life changed forever. It's a nightmare that is impossible to wake up from. Nothing can prepare us for such a loss. It leaves a path of devastation with emotions so intense there is no escaping them. It's such a lonely place, a place where you feel everything and nothing. I never knew how much a heart could hurt or how many tears could be shed. Time does not heal missing your child. It only gets worse. I still shake my head in disbelief every day. I still remember it like it was yesterday. It's difficult to wrap my head around that it has been this long since I sent him off to work that morning. He is missed terribly. He was such a great guy with the best personality. We miss you Tripp.

April 15th, 2021

I can't believe it's been 4075 days since Tripp went to Heaven. I remember having this picture taken. We were so happy and *zapp*. Tripp was gone. I miss him so much and it still seems he has to be here somewhere. I look for him every day. It may be in the clouds, the sun, the rain, or through my tears which flow daily. Some days are easy, some days are very tearful, but as far as I have traveled on this grief journey, I can't imagine not thinking and loving him every single day and missing him immensely. I pray for all of you several times a day.

Why Me? - Navigating the Unbearable Truth of Grief and Loss

February 17th, 2022

Today is twelve years. Twelve freaking years of not having my boy here with me. I had a really rough morning but as the afternoon came, I was feeling better. Now, not so much. I'm very sad and tearful all over again, and it's not the welling up of tears. It's the ones that gush and drip off your face that you didn't see coming. I cry at the drop of a hat anymore anyway, but these anniversaries are so very difficult. The worst day of my life. It's just so difficult to even wrap my mind around even twelve years later. I miss him so.

July 25th, 2022

As the group founder, owner, and grief counselor, I hesitate to post at times because I don't want our newcomers to think that our grief doesn't get better because it does. At the same time, some days, hours, or minutes knock the breath out of me. This is one of those nights. Tripp was killed twelve and a half years ago, and I have held his picture to my heart tonight and sobbed; I miss him so much every day. The years that have passed mean nothing. I love him more every day and miss him. Time is nothing but everything. Even though it still feels like yesterday, he was alive and well, my heart knows differently. The grief is softer, but it doesn't take away the intense love or heartache of not having him here with me. He was my buddy and I miss him.

February 17th, 2024

I write this with a heavy heart that I have had for 14 years, beginning February 17th at 7:26 am. Though it has been 14 years since Tripp's untimely passing, at times, it still feels as fresh as the day it happened.

The loss of a child is a tragedy that no parent should ever have to endure. No words can adequately describe the ache, the life once vibrant and full of joy that has been forever altered. My heart is filled with memories of Tripp, who once brought laughter, warmth, and an incredible sense of purpose. But now, all of that has faded away, replaced by a haunting silence.

Shirley Tripp Johnson

The milestones and anniversaries that should have been celebrated with joy now cast a shadow of sorrow. Special family gatherings are tinged with a bittersweet longing- a reminder of the person who should still be here but is forever absent. These occasions bring a mixture of both gratitude for the time spent together and profound sadness for the moments that will never be shared.

While time continues to move forward, I will carry the love of Tripp in my heart forever. It has become a part of who I am now, an eternal bond that can't be broken. The pain may soften over the years, but the love remains unchanged and unwavering.

Time does not heal the loss of a child. In my darkest moments, I find solace in the memories I hold dear. The laughter, the love, and the unique bond we shared are etched permanently in my heart. I am grateful for the time we had, but I can't help but yearn for more.

> ### Young Life Cut Short
>
> Do not judge a song by its duration
> Nor by the number of its notes
> Judge it by the way it touches
> and lifts the soul
> Sometimes those unfinished
> are among the most beautiful...
> And when something has
> enriched your life
> And when it's melody lingers
> on in your heart.
> Is it unfinished?
> Or is it endless?
>
> Unknown

Why Me? - Navigating the Unbearable Truth of Grief and Loss

Memories, however, are cherished; they serve as bittersweet reminders of what could have been, as well as a testament to the deep love I carry for Tripp. I know I will see him again in Heaven, and I am comforted by that, but I miss him so very much now. I will never forget February 17th, 2010. It is the worst day of my life. The day my life changed forever. I love you, Tripp and my broken heart misses you so much.

Can you take a moment to look back at some of my early thoughts on grief and compare them to how they evolved over the years? While intense sadness filled most of my journal entries, can you see through my writings that I was healing? My tone began to change as time passed. That's why I believe journaling is so important—writing your thoughts down allows you to track your journey. Often, we don't realize we're improving, but when we look back on our notes, we can see the progress we've made.

If you are struggling, try writing your thoughts down. Look back every now and then, and you will see that you, too, are making progress.

Chapter 10

Grace Through Grief

*Sometimes the greatest inspiration for living comes
when your mind is beyond the river
that doesn't have a bridge.*

~Shirley Tripp Johnson~

Even though I was traveling frequently for the retreats, it felt like I only truly *lived* when I was with other grievers. In those moments, I could pour out my heart and be met with understanding. But when I returned home, reality felt different—lonely and heavy.

There's something about the bond between parents who have experienced child loss that goes beyond words. No matter what you're feeling, it's just *understood*. I always looked forward to meeting up with another mom, especially during the week-long retreats and gatherings.

I truly believe that the retreats and spending weeks with other parents helped me grow and heal. Through all the struggles—the overwhelming sadness, the unbearable weight of grief—I've come to see myself as a survivor. I survived being so shattered and broken that I didn't think I could make it through another day, sometimes not even another hour. But I did. And you can, too. We all can.

If you're struggling, keep fighting—fight for the love. The love your child had for you, and you for them, is endless. They want you to find joy again and to live. No matter how long it takes, keep going. When you finally reach the other side of it, you'll know. That's when a whole new path begins, one filled with twists and turns, jagged edges, and unexpected drop-offs. But it's worth every single step, I promise you.

Why Me? - Navigating the Unbearable Truth of Grief and Loss

If you feel called to help others—do it. Don't be afraid. Not everyone is meant to do this work with the grieving, and it's not easy to bear another's sadness without letting it weigh you down. But some of us are built for this kind of work, while others aren't—and that's okay. What's important is that we all need one another.

Always reach out to someone new in their grief. Never doubt that you can make a difference, because you can. Sometimes, simply being there for someone is the greatest gift you can give.

When the pain feels unbearable and you think you can't go on, keep trying to find something positive each day. Work on shifting your thought patterns, even if it's just a little at a time. Each day you wake up is proof that you've made it through one more day. While sadness may linger for years to come, seek out moments of joy—no matter how small. They are there, waiting to be found.

Take frequent walks down memory lane, for it is there you will always find your child. Over time, the pain will begin to ease, and healing will gradually take place. It's a slow process, but allow yourself to go with it. Wherever your journey leads, let it guide you and sweep you into the places you need to go to begin healing. Even in the darkest moments, when it feels like you're lost, remember—those moments are part of your healing, even if it doesn't feel like it at the time.

You have to feel to heal. Embrace your emotions as you navigate this journey. Take time to work on yourself and look in the mirror often. You'll notice that you're changing, day by day. You'll never be the person you once were, and that's okay. You're becoming someone stronger, wiser, and even better.

I've learned that whatever traits defined you before tend to rise to the surface during grief. If you were a loving person, that love will shine even brighter. But if you harbor resentment or anger, those feelings may become even more pronounced. This is something you'll need to address, as it can hinder your healing process.

Start building connections as early as you can by joining online support groups, like those on Facebook, and sharing your story. Talk about your child to anyone willing to listen—doing so is a vital part of healing. Missing our children will never go away, nor would we want it to. Our love for them only grows stronger with each passing day because they will always be a part of us.

Some people may feel uncomfortable when you bring up a child who has passed, but gently remind them that you have every right to speak your child's name. Don't let anyone dictate how you should grieve. Those who haven't experienced the loss of a child are often the quickest to offer advice, but they can't truly understand—because even we don't fully understand this journey.

In the beginning, after losing a child, people often want us to "get over" our grief. I always say, "You need to let go of your desire for me to get over my grief. It's mine, not yours."

Fifteen years later, I have shared some of my raw emotions from when I was going through the depths of hell. I still mourn for Tripp every day, but I am better, and I know you will be too. I have to say, if it weren't for my husband Dan, and my children Jeremiah and Deidre, I don't think I could have made it through. Keeping them in my heart, especially when I didn't know if I would survive, kept me going, and now, all the friends I've made along this journey are treasures I will always cherish.

Grief drops a bomb into your life. You're shattered, torn apart, nearly destroyed. Amidst the fragments and debris, you somehow continue to exist. You don't know how you can't see the way forward. All you can do is feel the immense pain, both within and around you. You don't understand it, and you wonder if you ever will. You lie down in the rubble, unable to do anything else, and you cry—like you've never cried before. You ask yourself, why me? Why this?

Why Me? - Navigating the Unbearable Truth of Grief and Loss

And somehow, without knowing how, you begin to uncurl, wiping away more tears, and you start to walk. Slowly, you begin to gather the broken pieces of your life—one shard here, one there. They no longer fit together as they once did, and you realize there's no going back to what was. Yet, as each tiny fragment is reshaped, so are you. The new shape that emerges feels like a stranger, both to you and to others. But these broken pieces—this fractured self—have become you. They speak of your strength and your courage, and they tell the story of you: the vulnerable, the broken, the loving, the wonderful you.

One day, you, too, will have your own survival story. When I have a tough day now, I reflect on how the Lord has brought me through some incredibly difficult times, and I know He will continue to. So, when I experience sadness now, I understand that it's just part of the healing process. Even after fifteen years, I'm still being molded into a new version of myself.

As I sat down to piece together all my notes from over the years, I couldn't hold back the tears. Reading through the times when my grief was so deep that I didn't want to go on was overwhelming. My heart felt heavy as I revisited the desperation I had once felt. I'll never forget that kind of pain, and I wouldn't wish it on anyone.

But as I look back, I also see how far the good Lord has brought me. Through it all, He protected me and gave me courage, even when I didn't realize it. Without that courage, I don't think I would have made it. Over the past fifteen years, I've witnessed so many others enduring profound pain, and it's heartbreaking to see, but I have also seen them grow and heal as time went by and that is the blessing in all of this.

Reading my earlier feelings and thoughts, and writing the first few chapters was extremely difficult even fifteen years later. It reminded me of how desperate I once felt. But I thank God for the strength I found in thinking of my family—they saved my life. I've cried countless tears while writing this book, reliving everything all over again. Yet, I am profoundly grateful for the opportunity to share my story with you.

Shirley Tripp Johnson

My prayer is that, in some way, this book has shown you that you, too, can survive the most heartbreaking, earth-shattering event imaginable—the loss of a child. God bless you all, and thank you for reading my story.

A few things to remember:

- You have to feel to heal
- Don't have expectations of others
- Make your connections
- Tell your story over and over
- Find joy

And hey, here's something to always keep in mind: when you visit someone who's grieving, and they're clutching a tiny, crumpled Kleenex that's already soaked through with tears and snot—and they just keep wiping tear after tear and snot running like crazy-do them a favor. Get up and grab a roll of toilet paper, a box of tissues, or even a roll of paper towels. One little tissue isn't going to cut it, folks. They need the whole box.

Chapter 11

Headlines of Heartbreak

These are a few of the Newspaper Articles on the day of the accident and after. The articles show who they were written by. I know there is some redundancy with them but each one was written a little differently.

Family Devastated, Students Shaken After Bus Crash by Karen Araiza NBC Published February 17, 2010

A school bus and car collided in front of Perkiomen Valley Middle School West, Wednesday morning, killing one person who was in the car and injuring a second.

No one on the bus was seriously hurt -- five students with minor injuries were checked out at the scene by the school nurse, according to Michelle Brown, a spokeswoman for the school district. Sandra Myers said her daughter texted her just after 7:30 a.m. about the crash.

"She said they didn't really hit that hard and…everything was handled very carefully, professionally," said Sandra Myers, the mother of a student on the bus.

The car was in bad shape — it looked like it had been hit with a giant sledgehammer.

"It appears that the school bus attempted to turn left into the middle school in front of the path of the Honda Civic," said Lt. David Buckley of the Pa. State Police.

Frederick Poust, the 38-year-old bus driver, slowed to make a left turn into the school, police said.

The accident shut down Rt. 73 between Swamp Creek Rd. and Simmons Rd. as rescue crews worked to get to the two victims who were trapped inside the car.

Richard Taylor, 27, the car's passenger, was pronounced dead at the scene.

The car's driver, 41-year-old Freddy Carroll, was airlifted to Hahnemann Hospital to be treated for injuries that police said were serious but not life-threatening.

Taylor, whose nickname was Tripp, had just returned to the area after attending the University of Arkansas.

"You never think that your baby is going to be gone," said his mother, Shirley. "It's just not right because he had his whole life ahead of him."

"He just lights up everyone's life," said his father Dan.

The Johnsons hope accident investigators can find the cause of the crash, not to place blame, but to have closure.

Additional counselors were called into the school to help students cope.

Police: Bus driver involved in 1999 fatal crash By ABC7 Thursday, February 18, 2010

Frederick Poust III of Schwenksville was using his cell phone when he went through a stop sign at Route 152 and Rickert Road in November of 1999. His Ford Explorer slammed into a Jeep driven by Patricia Pena of Perkasie, Bucks County.

In the car was Patricia's 2-year-old daughter, Morgan, who died of injuries suffered in the accident.

Poust, who was 27 years old at the time and working as a volunteer fireman, was charged only with running a stop sign and careless driving. The Pena's subsequently launched a campaign to outlaw the use of hand-held cell phones while driving.

The latest accident occurred at approximately 7:25 a.m. Wednesday outside Perkiomen Valley Middle School West, located along Route 73 in Zieglerville.

Police say the bus, driven by a now 37-year-old Frederick Poust, was traveling west on Route 73. The bus entered the path of an oncoming Honda Civic while turning into the campus of Perkiomen Valley Middle School West.

The 27-seven-year-old passenger in the Honda, Richard "Tripp" Taylor of Gilbertsville, was pronounced dead at the scene.

Freddy Carroll, the 41-year-old driver of the car, was extricated from the vehicle and flown to Hahnemann Hospital for treatment. His injuries do not appear to be life-threatening. Police say he was conscious and alert upon leaving the scene.

Police say Carroll owns a small contracting company and Taylor was one of his employees.

Taylor's mother, Shirley Johnson, said the pair were builders and were on their way to a house they were renovating. She related a call from the home's owner who had learned of the crash.

"She got on the phone and said some kind words about Tripp. She said the house was a mess because of the renovation but whenever he walked in the whole room just lit up," Johnson said. "She was very grateful to have gotten to know him."

There were 45 children on the bus. Some suffered bumps and bruises and were treated by a school nurse at the scene. A district official said counselors are available to students who might need them.

The driver of the bus was uninjured and both he and the bus company, Student Transportation of America, have been fully cooperative with the investigation.

Locals told Action News they had long feared something terrible would happen at that intersection. There is no school crossing zone there, and the posted speed limit is 50 miles per hour.

Residents say it is risky for lumbering buses to turn across traffic.

'My broken heart is never going to heal'
By Carl Hessler Jr. The Pottstown Mercury
Published: April 5th, 2011

Rescuers at work trying to rescue Tripp from the passenger side of the car and his boss on the driver's side.

Recalling the "infectious" smile of her son, Shirley Johnson said her heart was forever broken by the crash that claimed her son's life.

"He was loved by everybody, everybody that met him. When he walked into the room, he just enlightened everybody. Everybody just kind of drew to him because of his infectious smile and just the way he held himself," a tearful Johnson said Monday, recalling her son Richard "Tripp" Taylor. "He was a very compassionate, loving individual and very close to his family."

Taylor, 27, of Gilbertsville, died Feb. 17, 2010, after a school bus recklessly operated by Frederick Poust III traveled into the path of a 1999 Honda Civic in which Taylor was a front seat passenger. Poust, traveling west on Route 73 in Lower Frederick turned left, attempting to enter Perkiomen Valley Middle School West, directly in front of the eastbound Honda, police said.

The driver of the Honda, Freddie Carroll, 41, of Perkiomenville, was seriously injured.

Johnson, also of Gilbertsville, was in court to witness Poust's admission to vehicular homicide in connection with her son's death. At the mention of her son's death in court, Johnson began to sob and had to be consoled by her husband, Dan, who was Richard's stepfather.

"It's a very sad day for me. A sad day because it brings back the reality that my son isn't going to be here anymore," said Johnson, her voice quivering with emotion. "No matter what the guilty plea, or whatever it is, it doesn't make me feel any better."

"He's never going to walk through the door again. My broken heart is never going to heal," added Johnson.

Johnson, who said she is a "compassionate" person, said "a million things" have been on her mind during this tragic period in her life.

"I know that I have to somehow or another find it in my heart to be forgiving also. Right now, I don't know when that's going to start because I'm still very, very hurt. It hurts every day," Johnson sobbed.

"There's not one moment, not one breath that I take, that I'm not thinking about Tripp, because he just brought so much joy to everybody that met him. We were very close. Knowing that he's never going to be here again, it just rips me apart."

Bus driver pleads guilty in fatal school bus-car crash
Published: April 5th, 2011 by Margaret Gibbons
Philadelphia Inquirer.

> The mother of the victim in a fatal school bus-car collision Monday said she was pleased to know that the bus driver will have to "face up to what he did."
>
> "But it is a very sad day for me, a sad day because it just brings back the reality that my son isn't going to be here anymore," said Shirley Johnson, the mother of Tripp Taylor, 27, of Gilbertsville.
>
> "My breaking heart will never heal," said Johnson, her voice breaking as she tried to control a sob. "This has been the worst year of my life."
>
> Shirley Johnson, mother of fatal bus-car collision Tripp Taylor, 27, speaks with reporters outside the courtroom after former school bus driver Frederick Poust, 39, pleads guilty to homicide by motor vehicle and related charges for causing the Feb. 17th, 2010

crash at the entrance to the Perkiomen Valley Middle School in Lower Frederick. Taylor was a passenger in the car. The man next to Mom is Taylor's step-dad

The mother of the victim in a fatal school bus-car collision Monday said she was pleased to know that the bus driver will have to "face up to what he did."

"But it is a very sad day for me, a sad day because it just brings back the reality that my son isn't going to be here anymore," said Shirley Johnson, the mother of Richard Taylor, 27, of Gilbertsville.

"My breaking heart will never heal," said Johnson, her voice breaking as she tried to control a sob. "This has been the worst year of my life."

Johnson's comments came in the wake of bus driver Frederick R. Poust III's admission in a Montgomery County courtroom Monday that he was driving recklessly when the bus collided with a car at the entranceway to Perkiomen Valley Middle School on Feb. 17, 2010. Taylor was a passenger in the car.

Poust, 39, of Schwenksville, pleaded guilty to a felony charge of homicide by motor vehicle and two misdemeanor charges of recklessly endangering the driver of the car, Freddie Carroll, 41, of Perkiomenville, as well as the 45 students on the bus at the time of the collision.

Poust entered an open guilty plea, which means there is no agreement on a sentence.

In 1999, Poust was talking on his cell phone when he was involved in an accident that killed 2 1/2-year-old Morgan Lee Pena in Hilltown. Poust pleaded guilty to two traffic violations in that case.

On Monday, Judge Joseph A. Smyth postponed sentencing on last year's fatality until the adult probation office can complete a presentence report on Poust's background.

Poust could be sentenced to a maximum of 5 1/2 to 11 years in prison and/or fined up to $25,000. State sentencing guidelines call for a minimum prison sentence of three to 12 months on the homicide by motor vehicle charge.

Johnson, flanked by the victim's stepfather, said she "absolutely" wants Poust to do jail time.

"Normally, I am a compassionate person," she said. "I know somehow or other I have to find it somewhere in my heart to be forgiving but, right now, I don't know when that is going to happen. It just rips me apart knowing my son is never going to be here again."

Johnson described Taylor as someone who would "light up a room and draw people to him with his infectious smile."

"He was a very compassionate, loving person," said Johnson.

Poust declined to comment when he left the courtroom as did defense attorney Brian J. McMonagle.

Deputy District Attorney Christopher M. Maloney said he first wants to review the presentence report before deciding on what type of sentence he will recommend for Poust.

"I would anticipate some jail would be appropriate under the circumstances," said Maloney.

"Mr. Poust has conceded he acted recklessly and negligently that day," said Maloney. "Not only did his actions result in the death of Mr. Taylor and permanent injuries to Mr. Carroll, but this crime reverberates through the community, making people question whether their children are safe when they are on a school bus. So, this crime has a profound impact not only on the immediate people involved but on the entire community."

Poust, delivering students to the middle school that morning, turned left to enter the school driveway without first stopping on the roadway and collided with the oncoming car that Carroll was driving.

Reviewing tapes from the bus's video system, investigators said the videos also showed Poust failing to come to a complete stop at 10 different stop signs before the accident.

In addition, authorities said the videos showed Poust displaying signs of fatigue, inattentiveness, and carelessness throughout the trip that morning. The videos captured Poust, who had a second job at night and had not slept for at least 24 hours before the accident, rubbing his eyes and face numerous times in the hour just before the crash, the criminal complaint said.

Poust had a second job working security from 10 p.m. to 6 a.m. at Souderton Mennonite Home. His last full sleep was on the night of Feb. 15 into the morning of Feb. 16, according to authorities.

Poust was using a cell phone on Nov. 3, 1999, when he blew through a stop sign in Hilltown and struck another vehicle in the intersection. Pena, the 2 1/2-year-old passenger in the other vehicle, died one day later from injuries she suffered in the accident. Poust pleaded guilty to two summary traffic violations, careless driving and going through a stop sign, for that accident.

The bus company that employed Poust, stating that Poust had all the proper credentials, knew of the citations but was not aware of the details of the 1999 incident.

Driver sentenced in 2010 Perk Valley school bus crash by "The Reporter, Montgomery Media" Published August 24, 2011

NORRISTOWN – A Schwenksville man remained stone-faced as a judge sent him to jail for recklessly driving a school bus and failing to yield to an oncoming car, striking it and killing a Gilbertsville man who was a passenger in the car.

Frederick Robert Poust III, 39, of Mine Hill Road, was sentenced Thursday in Montgomery County Court to 1 to 2 years in the county jail, to be followed by five years' probation, after he pleaded guilty to charges of homicide by vehicle and recklessly endangering other persons in connection with the 7:26 a.m. Feb. 17, 2010, crash outside Perkiomen Valley Middle School West on Route 73 in Lower Frederick.

Killed in the two-vehicle crash was Richard "Tripp" Taylor, 27, who was a passenger in the 1999 Honda Civic that was struck by the bus. The driver of the Honda, Freddie Carroll, 41, of Perkiomenville, was seriously injured in the crash.

"I don't think any sentence would have been long enough. Nothing is going to bring back Tripp, but I respect the judge's decision," Johnson, clutching a photograph of her son, said after the hearing. "Tripp was an amazing son and brother and he loved his family. He was just a very compassionate person."

Carroll, who walked to court with a cane as a result of leg injuries he suffered in the crash, indicated he would have liked to have seen more jail time for Poust.

Judge Joseph A. Smyth, who imposed the punishment during an emotional hearing, also ordered Poust to complete 200 hours of community service as a condition of the sentence.

Why Me? - Navigating the Unbearable Truth of Grief and Loss

Poust automatically loses his driver's license for three years as a result of the conviction. The judge further ordered that before Poust's driving privileges are ever restored, he is to complete a safe driving course.

Taylor's mother, Shirley Johnson, and Carroll were in the courtroom as the sentence was imposed.

"I'm disappointed with the sentence. I think a man who kills a dog gets more time than that man for killing my friend. But I guess that's the sentence," Carroll said outside the courtroom.

Earlier, Carroll told the judge he still relives "the horrible tragedy of watching my friend get killed this way," but added he has tried to forgive Poust.

Before learning his fate, Poust addressed Johnson and Carroll in the packed courtroom.

"I do apologize for your loss. I think about this accident every day," said Poust, a father of two who was supported in court by several relatives, including his mother.

Under state sentencing guidelines Poust faced an average sentence of 3-to-12 months in jail for the vehicular homicide conviction.

Deputy District Attorney Christopher Maloney sought a sentence closer to the top of the guidelines.

Maloney argued Poust's involvement in a fatal crash that killed a 2-year-old girl 10 years ago, "suggests he should have been cognizant of the risks of being inattentive and careless while you drive." Maloney also referred to the moments leading up to the fatal crash when Poust failed to completely stop at 10 separate stop signs during his bus route while carrying 45 students.

"The way he drove on that morning shows his experience (10 years ago) ...had no impact on him and he continued to drive recklessly and carelessly," Maloney argued, adding such a crash "causes us to question how safe we are as we go about our daily routines."

Defense lawyer Brian J. McMonagle sought a sentence closer to the bottom of the guideline range.

"He is remorseful and has accepted responsibility. I could go on and on about all the goodness that's there," said McMonagle, arguing Poust lived a life based on community service, including working as a volunteer firefighter.

Poust's relatives described him as a "caring, warm, compassionate, soft-spoken and quiet man" who was more like a "big teddy bear."

With his guilty plea, Poust conceded that his recklessness and negligence caused Taylor's death and that he endangered the lives of Carroll and the 45 students on the bus.

The investigation determined the 2005 Blue Bird school bus was traveling west on Route 73 and turned left, attempting to enter the school complex, directly in front of the eastbound Honda operated by Carroll.

Poust was not injured. Five students on the bus suffered minor injuries, police said.

After the crash, Poust allegedly told detectives, "I slowed down to enter the turning lane and came to a complete stop in the turning lane." Poust claimed that before he attempted to turn, he stopped for "a few seconds," according to the arrest affidavit.

However, the bus, court papers indicate, was equipped with an onboard video system consisting of four separate camera angles to capture the bus' movement as well as the interior and exterior of the bus during its operation.

Investigators reviewed video footage and determined Poust did not stop before attempting his left turn into the school complex and "encroached into the path of the oncoming Honda," according to the arrest affidavit.

The video footage also showed Poust displaying signs of fatigue, inattentiveness, and carelessness throughout the morning of the fatal crash, authorities alleged.

Investigators determined Poust last had a full night's sleep on the evening of Monday, Feb. 15 into Tuesday morning Feb. 16, according to court papers. Poust allegedly told authorities he had a second job working nights from 10 p.m. to 6 a.m.

The driver handbook for Student Transportation of America Inc., the company for which Poust once worked, requires drivers to report to work "in a fit, rested condition," according to the criminal complaint.

Furthermore, authorities alleged, that while Poust was not talking on a cell phone at the time of the crash, he did have a hands-free device in his right ear and had talked to a female friend while operating the bus earlier that morning.

Poust also was observed using an electronic music device with a portable speaker system while the bus was in operation with students on board, authorities alleged.

Electronic devices such as radios and MP3 players, and the use of headphones and earbuds "are not permitted" under the bus company's driver handbook, according to court documents.

Blood tests determined that drugs and alcohol were not factors in the crash.

Montco man gets jail time in fatal school bus crash By Carl Hessler Published August 25th, 2011

A Schwenksville man is headed to jail after admitting that he recklessly drove a school bus and failed to yield to an oncoming car, striking it and killing a Gilbertsville man who was a passenger in the car.

Frederick Robert Poust III, 39, of Mine Hill Road, was sentenced Thursday in Montgomery County Court to 1 to 2 years in the county jail, to be followed by five years' probation, after he pleaded guilty to charges of homicide by vehicle and recklessly endangering other persons in connection with the 7:26 a.m. Feb. 17, 2010, crash

Shirley Tripp Johnson

outside Perkiomen Valley Middle School West on Route 73 in Lower Frederick.

Killed in the two-vehicle crash was Richard "Tripp" Taylor, 27, who was a passenger in a 1999 Honda Civic that was struck by the school bus. The driver of the Honda, Freddie Carroll, 41, of Perkiomenville, was seriously injured in the crash.

Judge Joseph A. Smyth, who imposed the punishment during an emotional sentencing hearing, also ordered Poust to complete 200 hours of community service.

With the guilty plea, Poust conceded that his recklessness and negligence caused Taylor's death and that he endangered the lives of Carroll and the 45 students on the bus.

The investigation determined the 2005 Blue Bird school bus was traveling west on Route 73 and turned left, attempting to enter the school complex, directly in front of the eastbound Honda operated by Carroll.

Poust was not injured. Five students on the bus suffered minor injuries, police said.

After the crash, Poust allegedly told detectives, "I slowed down to enter the turning lane and came to a complete stop in the turning lane." Poust claimed that before he attempted to turn, he stopped for "a few seconds," according to the arrest affidavit.

However, the bus, court papers indicate, was equipped with an onboard video system consisting of four separate camera angles to capture the bus' movement as well as the interior and exterior of the bus during its operation.

Investigators reviewed video footage and determined Poust did not stop before attempting his left turn into the school complex and "encroached into the path of the oncoming Honda," according to the arrest affidavit.

The video footage also showed Poust displaying signs of fatigue, inattentiveness, and carelessness throughout the morning of the fatal crash, authorities alleged.

Investigators determined Poust last had a full night's sleep on the evening of Monday, Feb. 15 into Tuesday morning Feb. 16, according to court papers. Poust allegedly told authorities he had a second job working nights from 10 p.m. to 6 a.m.

The driver handbook for Student Transportation of America Inc., the company for which Poust worked, requires drivers to report to work "in a fit, rested condition," according to the criminal complaint.

While reviewing the bus' videotape, authorities determined Poust, while driving his assigned school bus route that morning, "failed to come to a complete stop at posted stop signs" on 10 separate occasions between 6:39 a.m. and 7:17 a.m., according to the arrest affidavit.

Furthermore, authorities alleged, that while Poust was not talking on a cell phone at the time of the crash, he did have a hands-free device in his right ear and had talked to a female friend while operating the bus earlier that morning.

Poust also was observed using an electronic music device with a portable speaker system while the bus was in operation with students on board, authorities alleged.

Electronic devices such as radios and MP3 players, and the use of headphones and earbuds "are not permitted" under the bus company's driver handbook, according to court documents.

Blood tests determined that drugs and alcohol were not factors in the crash.

August 25th, 2011 Carl *Hessler Jr. on Twitter @MontcoCourtNews*

NORRISTOWN – "It's a beautiful day, mama. It's a beautiful day. I love you."

Those words, the last her son Richard "Tripp" Taylor uttered to her hours before he died in a crash, still echo in Shirley Johnson's mind and fill her heart with sadness.

Shirley Tripp Johnson

"I was a normal mother that day. Now, I'm a grieving mother," a tearful Johnson said Thursday, recalling her last moments with her 27-year-old son.

Taylor, of Gilbertsville, died about 7:26 a.m. Feb. 17, 2010, after a school bus recklessly operated by Frederick Poust III traveled into the path of a 1999 Honda Civic in which Taylor was a front seat passenger. Poust, traveling west on Route 73 in Lower Frederick turned left, attempting to enter Perkiomen Valley Middle School West, directly in front of the eastbound Honda, police said.

"Every morning, I would make Tripp's lunch. That morning was like any other, I made his lunch and he came bouncing down the stairs as usual with a big smile on him," Johnson, also of Gilbertsville, recalled. "He took his lunch, leaned over and gave me a hug and a kiss and told me he loved me and to have a good day."

Shirley Johnson holds a photo of her son while she talks about losing him in a car crash.
Photo from video by Carl Hessler Jr.

"He always stopped at the door when he opened it and kind of threw his chest out and put his nose in the air and sniffed and said, 'It's a beautiful day, mama.' He always did that every morning," Johnson affectionately recalled. "I always waved at him until he was out of sight."

The grief still obvious in her voice, Johnson said Tripp's death has affected all aspects of her life.

Why Me? - Navigating the Unbearable Truth of Grief and Loss

"My heart aches as his mom that I wasn't able to save him. I'm having to live all over again with a broken heart," said Johnson, recalling the son who had a boisterous laugh, loved to sing the Wawa hoagie jingle and wear strong cologne.

Johnson, who attended Poust's sentencing hearing, had to be consoled at times by her husband, Dan, who was Richard's stepfather, and other relatives.

"No more hugs. No more, 'I love you mama.' He is dead. My baby boy is dead," said Johnson, her voice quivering with emotion. "I did not choose this life sentence for myself. Mr. Poust did that for me."

Recalling the "infectious" laugh of her son, Johnson, clutching a photograph of Tripp with his brother Jeremiah and sister Deidre during happier times, said her heart was forever broken by the crash that claimed her son's life.

"Walk into a room and all eyes would turn toward Tripp because he'd have a huge, bright white smile and have a laugh that everyone just caught on to. Everyone loved Tripp, he had a lot of friends. He's going to be missed by many," Johnson said.

Deidre Taylor-Schlegel, Tripp's sister, said her children have been robbed of their uncle, who adored them.

"Our lives have been robbed of so many memories," Taylor-Schlegel said.

Jeremiah Shinn, Tripp's brother, added his brother had a positive view of the world and compassion for everyone.

"He had far more to teach me than I could ever teach him," Shinn said.

Johnson indicated she is trying to turn her grief into something positive. Since Tripp's death, she returned to school to study grief therapy and counseling and wants to begin helping other bereaved parents.

"There's just a very strong need to educate everybody about bereavement when you've lost a child. Time does not heal when you lose a child," Johnson said. "I just want to make sure people are educated, that you can grieve healthy. As hard as it is, as long as you take one breath at a time and one step in front of the other, we'll get through this together as bereaved parents and we're there to support each other."

Montco School Bus Driver Sentenced For 2010 Fatal Crash CBS Philadelphia: Published August 25th, 2011

(CBS) – A Montgomery County, Pa. man who ignited a national debate more than a decade ago about cell phone use while driving will spend at least a year behind bars for causing a deadly crash last year while driving a school bus loaded with children.

The judge today sentenced Frederick Poust III to one to two years in jail followed by five years' probation after the 39-year-old man pleaded guilty to charges of vehicular homicide and reckless endangerment.

The Schwenksville, Pa. man admitted he was negligent when he turned into the path of oncoming traffic in front of the Perkiomen Valley Middle School last year, hitting a car and killing the passenger, Richard "Tripp" Taylor.

"I don't think any sentence would have been long enough," said Taylor's mother, Shirley Johnson, after the sentencing. "Nothing's going to bring back Tripp. But I respect the judge's decision, and we just go from there."

The onboard video shows Poust rolling through stop signs while talking on the cell phone and listening to loud music.

More than a decade ago, the same man had killed a two-year-old girl in Bucks County when he ran a stop sign while dialing a phone. He was not criminally charged in that accident.

Bus driver jailed for fatal crash. Margaret Gibbons Philadelphia Inquirer Published: August 26th, 2011

Why Me? - Navigating the Unbearable Truth of Grief and Loss

A Schwenksville man 10 years ago received two traffic citations for a fatal accident that resulted in the death of a 2 ½-year-old girl in Hilltown.

But Frederick R. Poust III, 39, of the 800 block of Mine Hill Road, received jail time Thursday for his second fatal accident, this one occurring when the school bus he was driving crashed into a car in February 2010.

Montgomery County Judge Joseph A. Smyth Thursday sentenced Poust to one to two years in the county prison.

Poust, who showed no emotion on learning his fate, also will have to serve a five-year probation sentence, perform 200 hours of community service, and pay $21,153 in restitution.

That was not good enough for 42-year-old Perkiomenville resident Freddie Carroll, the driver of the car that was involved in the collision with the school bus.

"I am disappointed with the sentence," said Carroll after Poust was taken from the courtroom in handcuffs by deputies to begin serving his sentence at the county prison.

"I think a man who kills a dog gets more time than that man got for killing my friend," said Carroll, who now walks with a cane after suffering a severely damaged right leg in the accident.

The crash occurred on the morning of Feb. 17, 2010, when the bus that Poust was driving which contained 45 students crashed into Carroll's 1999 Honda Civic at the entranceway to the Perkiomen Valley Middle School West in Lower Frederick.

The passenger in the car, Richard Taylor, 27, of Gilbertsville, was pronounced dead at the scene from head injuries he suffered in the accident.

"Time does not heal when you lose a child," testified Shirley Johnson, Taylor's mother, at the sentencing hearing.

Shirley Tripp Johnson

She said she still has those "choking moments" when she wakes up in the middle of the night thinking about the wrecked car and her son taking his last breath in that car.

Attempting to explain the impact of the loss of the youngest of her three children, Johnson used a series of "Nevers" _ never again having to buy "boatloads of cereal," never seeing him marry and have children of his own, never again hearing him sing the Wawa hoagie song.

And, showing the judge an enlarged photo of a smiling Taylor with his older brother and sister, Johnson told the judge there would never again be a family photo depicting her three children together.

"There will be no more Tripp hugs, no more Tripp smiles," said Johnson. "He is dead. He is dead. My baby boy is dead."

Johnson also said she quickly learned that the only solace she could find often came from other bereaved parents because "society does not want to hear about our dead children." Her experience has motivated her to return to school to be licensed in grief therapy and counseling to offer help to grieving parents who may otherwise be unable to afford it.

"Grief knows no bounds," said Johnson. "A broken heart cripples you but you have to learn to live life differently."

Two of Michael Dubinski's daughters were on the bus that fatal day. His youngest, who was 11 at the time, suffered a stomach injury and bruise to her face and, while she recovered from her physical injuries, the emotional scars remain, Dubinski said.

His daughter still wakes up in tears, hearing the panicked screams of her fellow students on the bus that day as well as Carroll's terrifying screams for help, he said.

"Mr. Poust killed my daughter's innocence," Dubinski testified. "I will never forgive him for what he did to my youngest daughter."

Poust's family and friends described him as a warm, compassionate man, a good father and son, "a teddy bear."

"I do apologize for your loss," Poust said in an emotionless voice, turning to Johnson and her family. "I never intended to hurt anyone including the kids on my bus."

State sentencing guidelines recommended that Poust receive a minimum sentence of between three to 12 months on the homicide by motor vehicle charge to which he pleaded guilty in April and probation to three months minimum sentence on each of the two recklessly endangering others charges to which he pleaded.

County Deputy District Attorney Christopher M. Maloney argued for a sentence at the high end of the guidelines, claiming that Poust of all people should have been aware of the risks of inattentive driving because of the earlier fatal accident in which he was involved.

Defense attorney Brian J. McMonagle sought a sentence in the low end, noting that Poust suffers from stage four kidney disease and is on the kidney transplant list.

The judge said that, before his sentencing, he checked with county prison officials and was assured that the staff could handle Poust's medical condition even if he had to go on kidney dialysis during his incarceration.

The bus accident happened when Poust, delivering students to the middle school that morning, turned left to enter the school driveway without first stopping on the road. The bus crashed into the oncoming car that Carroll was driving.

Reviewing tapes from the bus' video system, investigators said the videos showed Poust failing to come to a complete stop at 10 different stop signs before the accident.

In addition, authorities said, the videos showed Poust displaying signs of fatigue, inattentiveness, and carelessness throughout that trip that morning. The videos captured Poust, who had a second job at night and had not slept for at least 24 hours before the accident, rubbing his eyes and face numerous times in the hour just before the crash, the criminal complaint said.

Poust had a second job working security from 10 p.m. to 6 a.m. at the Souderton Mennonite Home. His last full sleeping period was on the night of Feb. 15, 2010, into the morning of Feb. 16, 2010, according to authorities.

This was the second fatal accident that Poust was accused of initiating.

Poust was using a cell phone on Nov. 3, 1999, when he blew through a stop sign in Hilltown, Bucks County, and struck another vehicle in the intersection. Morgan Lee Pena, the 2 ½-year-old passenger in the other vehicle, died one day later from injuries she suffered in the accident. Poust, a Quakertown resident at the time, pleaded guilty to two summary traffic violations, careless driving and going through a stop sign, for that accident.

Officials of the bus company that employed Poust said Poust had all the proper credentials. Also, while they said they knew of the two traffic citations, they said they were not aware of the details of the 1999 incident.

The Montgomery County district attorney's office, working with a bipartisan coalition of state lawmakers from the area, last summer was instrumental in getting the state Department of Transportation to provide more detailed driving history information on prospective bus drivers before their hiring.

Bus driver in fatal crash eligible for work release
Published by Margaret Gibbons, March 1st, 2012

A survivor of a fatal 2010 accident involving a school bus and a car on Thursday said he is "outraged" that the bus driver, who is serving a prison sentence for causing the accident, is now eligible for work release.

"The prison sentence already was too light," said 43-year-old Perkiomenville resident Freddie Carroll. "You get more time if you kill a dog. This is just another slap in the face to me and to the family (of the deceased victim)."

Why Me? - Navigating the Unbearable Truth of Grief and Loss

Carroll, who suffered severe leg damage in the collision, was responding to an order signed this week by Montgomery County Judge Joseph A. Smyth making Frederick R. Poust III eligible for work release.

Poust, 40, of the 800 block of Mine Hill Road, Schwenksville, was sentenced last August. He received one to two years in the county lockup after pleading guilty to homicide by motor vehicle for the death of Richard Taylor, 27, of Gilbertsville, and recklessly endangering others, including the 45 students on his bus, and Carroll, the driver of the car.

Poust also received a five-year probation sentence that will begin after he completes his parole time. He was further ordered to perform 200 hours of community service and to pay $21,152 in restitution.

Poust, in his petition to be made eligible for work release, said he is a "faithful servant of God," who goes to church each day, has never used drugs, and is not a flight risk.

While accepting full responsibility for his actions on that fatal day, Poust said in his petition that he has been a model prisoner and has completed various self-improvement programs offered at the prison.

Poust said he needs to get a job to help his family which includes his wife and two children, one who is 8 and another who is just 10 months old. His wife is struggling to support the family in his absence.

Also, the quicker he begins to work, the quicker he can begin to start paying restitution and court costs, according to the Poust petition.

Poust said he has talked to a prison chaplain about getting a job at one of the thrift stores owned by the chaplain's church. The chaplain has promised to help him find a job once he is made eligible for work release, according to Poust's petition.

County Deputy District Attorney Christopher M. Maloney said that, while not asked for any input on Poust's request, he deferred to Smyth's judgment in the matter.

Shirley Tripp Johnson

During conversations with the judge before Poust entered an open guilty plea to the charges, the issue of work release was brought up by Poust's defense attorney. The judge said that he would consider the request after Poust served at least six months in jail without getting into any disciplinary problems.

Maloney said that Carroll and the victim's family were made aware that work release was always a possibility.

Under the work release program, Poust will be allowed out of prison to go to a job but will have to return every night and remain in jail on days when he is not working.

"I just don't understand this," said Carroll. "There are good people out there who have committed no crimes but can't get a job while someone is willing to hire this man, who killed two people in his lifetime. It just makes no sense to me."

"I hope someone makes sure that he pays restitution with the money he will be earning," said Carroll, adding he had out-of-pocket expenses totaling almost $10,000 as a result of the accident.

The crash occurred on the morning of Feb. 17, 2010, when the bus that Poust was driving which contained 45 students crashed into Carroll's 1999 Honda Civic at the entrance to the Perkiomen Valley Middle School West in Lower Frederick.

Taylor, who was a passenger in Carroll's car, was pronounced dead at the scene from head injuries he suffered in the accident.

The bus accident happened when Poust, delivering students to the middle school that morning, turned left to enter the school driveway without first stopping on the road. The bus crashed into the oncoming car that Carroll was driving.

Reviewing tapes from the bus' video system, investigators said the videos showed Poust failing to come to a complete stop at 10 different stop signs before the accident.

In addition, authorities said, the videos showed Poust displaying signs of fatigue, inattentiveness, and carelessness throughout the trip that morning. The videos captured Poust, who had a second job at night and had not slept for at least 24 hours before the accident, rubbing his eyes and face numerous times in the hour just before the crash, the criminal complaint said.

Poust had a second job working security from 10 p.m. to 6 a.m. at the Souderton Mennonite Home. His last full sleeping period was on the night of Feb. 15, 2010, into the morning of Feb. 16, 2010, according to authorities.

This was the second fatal accident that Poust was accused of initiating.

Poust was using a handheld cell phone while driving a car on Nov. 3, 1999, when he went through a stop sign in Hilltown and struck another vehicle in the intersection. Morgan Lee Pena, the 2½-year-old passenger in the other vehicle, died one day later from injuries she suffered in the accident.

Poust, a Quakertown resident at the time, pleaded guilty to two summary traffic violations, careless driving and going through a stop sign, for that accident.

Officials of the bus company that employed Poust said Poust had all the proper credentials. Also, while they said they knew of the two traffic citations, they said they were not aware of the details of the 1999 incident.

The Montgomery County district attorney's office, working with a bipartisan coalition of state lawmakers from the area, subsequently was instrumental in getting the state Department of Transportation to provide more detailed driving history information on prospective bus drivers before their hiring.

Two Years After Son's Death, Montgomery County Mother Opens Grief Center Published by Walt Huner-CBS News. February 14th, 2010

MONTGOMERY COUNTY, Pa. (CBS) –A Montgomery County mother who lost her son in a car crash two years ago this week is now reaching out in a special way to help other bereaved parents.

Shirley Tripp Johnson

Shirley Johnson, whose 27-year-old son Tripp died on February 17, 2010, will open the "Wings of Hope" Grief Center tomorrow.

Johnson, who has decorated the meeting room with puffy clouds and angel wings, says she hopes to offer, in her words, a "cup of courage" to grieving parents who seek counseling with her.

Tripp died when the car he was riding in was rammed by a school bus. The driver of the school bus, who is now serving a prison sentence, was seen blowing past ten stop signs before the bus—loaded with 45 children—was involved in the fatal crash.

Johnson, who says for months after Tripp's death she was overwhelmed by grief, studied hard to get her certification as a grief counselor in just nine months.

Gilbertsville Mom opens Grief Center. Published by Carl Hessler Jr., February 14, 2012

A grieving mother has turned tragedy into hope by offering what she calls 'a cup of courage' to others who are grieving the loss of loved ones.

Two years after her 27-year-old son, Richard 'Tripp' Taylor, died in a crash involving a school bus, Shirley Johnson, of Gilbertsville, is opening the 'Wings of Hope Grief Counseling and Support Center' at Route 100 and Grosser Road to provide grief support to others traveling the journey of grief.

Her son, who uttered to her, 'It's a beautiful day, mama,' just hours before he died in the crash, is her inspiration.

'He was a happy-go-lucky guy and all he ever wanted to do was to reach out and help people,' Johnson, her voice quivering with emotion at times, said as she recalled her son and the birth of her idea to start a grief counseling support center. 'I thought I should do something because there are people out there who need support in their grief no matter what their loss is. So that's what prompted me because I knew that people needed that immediate support.'

Why Me? - Navigating the Unbearable Truth of Grief and Loss

Taylor, of Gilbertsville, died about 7:26 a.m. Feb. 17, 2010, after a school bus recklessly operated by Frederick Poust III, who is now serving a jail sentence for the crash, traveled into the path of a 1999 Honda Civic in which Taylor was a front seat passenger. Poust, traveling west on Route 73 in Lower Frederick turned left, attempting to enter Perkiomen Valley Middle School West, directly in front of the eastbound Honda, police said.

'I was in a dark place for quite a few months after Tripp got killed because there was nobody that I knew that had lost a child. I thought I was going crazy because grief just wreaks havoc over your entire mind and body. It's horrible and it takes you down into the pits of hell,' Johnson recalled. 'It's the darkest place a person could ever be.'

'If I would have just had someone that had lost a child come to me and let me know that how I was feeling was OK and these are the things that you're going to experience before you start to get better, I think that I would have never gone into that darkness as far as I did,' Johnson added.

Feeling 'numb, crazy, and angry' along with the pain, Johnson joined an online grief group and met a few parents who also had lost children. However, after having no luck trying to find a support group that was a fit, Johnson decided to start her own and developed an online support group.

After careful consideration, Johnson returned to school to become a certified grief counselor and achieved her goal in November.

'Now, I know that through the loss of my youngest son Tripp, I can help others on this horrible grief journey we must travel after the loss of a loved one,' Johnson said.

Johnson, a mother of three and Nana to four, plans to offer individual counseling sessions by appointment only and other grief support group meetings several times a week, specifically addressing the loss of a child or the loss of a loved one. Johnson is also planning 'Care and Share' meetings to be held on Sunday afternoons as well as a grief book exchange program through the center. Some

Shirley Tripp Johnson

insurance programs that cover grief counseling will be accepted for the center's services.

Johnson said the center, which has a meeting room decorated with angelic accents and clouds in a soothing, comfortable atmosphere, provides a healing place for those who experienced loss and provides resources to help them during the grieving process. The center is located on the third floor of a converted barn. 'Our purpose is to offer understanding, suggestions for coping, support, friendship, and most of all hope for all who are struggling with grief,' Johnson said.

'There's just a very strong need to educate everybody about bereavement when you've lost a child. Time does not heal when you lose a child. The grief never goes away,' Johnson said. 'There's no moving on. What I call it is living forward.'

'I just want to make sure people are educated, that you can grieve healthy. As hard as it is, as long as you take one breath at a time and one step in front of the other, we'll get through this together as bereaved parents, and we're there to support each other,' Johnson said.

'I know he would be proud because he was all about helping other people. He and I were a lot alike. The way Tripp lived his life, I guess I've tried to model some of that in my own life because he was so upbeat and so supportive of people who needed help. He was always giving of himself,' said Johnson, recalling the man who had an 'infectious' smile, a boisterous laugh, loved to sing the Wawa hoagie jingle, and wore strong cologne.

'Now, in his death, I want to be more like him because he was just such an amazing guy,' Johnson said.

Thank you for taking the time to read through these articles. I know some were redundant, but each one was a little different.

REVIEWS

I could write a book full of what others have said but here are just a few.

The following reviews were taken from a website, Great Non-Profits, and most of the reviews were regarding the retreats and the impact they had on the attendees. It's all about the connections.

https://greatnonprofits.org/organizations/view/wings-of-hope-living-forward-inc

Client Served

I lost my precious son Adam on 10/9/11 and found this group shortly after. Shirley and her group have been there for me every step of the way. I don't know how I would have survived my loss without her kind and caring support and love. This non-profit is amazing. After losing my husband on 9/21/17 Shirley stepped up to the plate and was again there to support me. The picture is of my son Adam and my husband John. Forever missed, forever loved. Thank you to Wings of Hope Living Forward Inc. for always being there for me and for all of the other grieving moms, dads, and grandparent. You are one in a million.

Client Served

Wings of Hope Living Forward is an amazing organization for grieving moms & dads. I found this group almost a decade ago after losing my second son. I made lifelong friends from Wings of Hope as I navigated child loss for the second time. Shirley Johnson & this group helped me find joy again even though I thought that would never be possible. I've attended many of the retreats & learned so much about the complicated nature of grief. I don't know where I would be today without this group of amazing men & women. We are warriors!!

Why Me? - Navigating the Unbearable Truth of Grief and Loss

Client Served

Wings of Hope has been a God-send for me! I have been a member of this organization almost since its inception. After losing my youngest son, Jess, in 2009 I found Wings of Hope quite by accident. I attended the first retreat held in 2013 & found a group of caring moms & dads who were on this same journey of navigating life without their precious children. I formed immediate bonds with the founder of the group & other members. Life-long friendships have been made at retreats & through the Facebook groups. These people literally held me up when I could not stand on my own. The retreats are wonderful & each one brought healing & hope for this brokenhearted mom. I truly can't say enough about how generous founder, Shirley Tripp Johnson is, both with her time & the efforts she puts into this organization. I tell every new grieving mom I meet about Wings of Hope. 10 years since the death of my precious Jess, I now share the group with excitement instead of sadness. I owe much of my healing to Wings of Hope (after God, of course)!!

Client Served

Somehow, I came across Wings of Hope. Went on my first retreat to Virginia Beach. I didn't know what to expect (I'm from the UK) I Found some amazing people, so friendly and welcoming (even though they couldn't understand my way of talking.) I made a special friend there, whom I have met several times since. I am forever grateful that I found Wings of Hope.

Client Served

This group has been my biggest blessing, Shirley Tripp-Johnson reached out to me as I was in another grieving group that was full of drama. No grieving mothers needs more drama or disagreements. I was removed from that group by the owner because we disagreed on all the drama. It just added to the stress and no support for understanding the outcry of grief. My heart would just hurt for the ones who were bullied in that group. Shirley Tripp-Johnson saw that I was lost again and invited me into her world of how to handle grieving mothers. What stage their UNBEARABLE pain was.

Shirley Tripp Johnson

Shirley Tripp-Johnson's group was well aware of what was happening in her group with so many grieving parents and grandparents. No drama is tolerated. You can voice your hurt and true feelings but not bash another who feels differently. Be kind with words of support. Shirley Tripp-Johnson is a blessing to many and a true supporter. I went to a grieving mother's retreat and met some mothers. These grieving mothers will always have a strong bond. These retreats are amazing! I can truly say I love these ladies I met at the retreat as forever sister. The cost is outstanding for all the support and bonding you leave with. And the star of these retreats are our children. " If you ever get a chance to go to one, please do! Shirley Tripp-Johnson thank you for all you do for the brokenhearted. Always my sister because of our Heavenly Children

Client Served

I just like to say finding this group has been the biggest help in dealing with the loss of my only son. I thought I was going to go crazy because I had no one to share what I was feeling with. I tried to reach out to get therapy, but I was put on a waiting list, and months went by with no contact from them, so that made me feel more alone. But here I found out what I was feeling was normal, that there is a process to this journey. This group has made me so much stronger, and for that, I will always be grateful.

Client Served

I went on a search for groups because I felt alone because I lost my mama the year before of cancer; I came across wings of hope moving forward and went to my first retreat in Smokey Mountains. It was the best decision I ever made!! This group is amazing and has helped so much with my grieving process, and I have made a new family with all of them. I love them dearly. They work so hard and give their heart with everything they do with these retreats!! We get so many gifts and have so many memories at these retreats. Without them, I would probably be locked up in a hospital. My daughter is my world, and when she entered heaven, I was lost!!! I want to thank Wings of Hope moving forward for the hope I have now to move forward for my 2 sons and not to give up!! Without all of you, I will still be so

Why Me? - Navigating the Unbearable Truth of Grief and Loss

lost!! Thank you for all the support and love you have shared with all of us.

Client Served

I can't put into words how truly important this organization is to support bereaved parents. Thank God & all those who are left here on this earth to help gain insight into our broken paths. As grieving parents, we feel we walk alone. Thank you!

Client Served

Wings of Hope has proven over and over to be a wonderful organization for bereaved parents. This organization truly allows you to be free in your grief without judgment. You are able to connect with people time and time again and develop amazing friendships with people who understand the tragedy of losing a child. This group has the most loving, compassionate, empathetic men and women you could ever meet. Each and every person I met has been a true inspiration and has left a deep impression on my heart.

Client Served

I found out that an online group I was recently a member of, got together for retreats a few times a year. At that point, all I could think about was joining my son, I just wanted to stay in bed till I died! My husband and I took our income tax that year and paid for a retreat. They were out of sponsorship funding at that time. At the retreat, I learned that most of my thoughts and feelings were shared by other parents there. We not only grieved together, but we laughed too! We are in a setting that requires us to be with each other, talking, therapy groups led by one of the founders Shirley who is a licensed grief counselor. As well as discussions led by our spiritual guru (lol) Renee. We do many group activities, an excursion or two, usually in a beautiful mansion on the beach! I feel like I woke up and was thawing, I was learning to live again, to find purpose out of my terrible sadness!

Shirley Tripp Johnson

Now, almost 3 years later, I'm doing fundraising here in Kentucky, to help send parents to these amazing retreats with Wings of Hope Living Forward. Their purpose to me is about saving lives! They saved mine!

Client Served

After the death of my only son, I was so lost in grief and the pain had become unbearable! Counseling helped very little, as I later understood that unless you've lost a child...then how can you truly empathize and understand the pain and daily struggles just to get out of bed?

By chance, I found this group online that offered support through sharing our pain, experiences, strength, and hope! The group was so loving and supportive, and so many parents were reaching out to each other...because it was okay to bare your soul on there, without judgment, ridicule, or being abandoned...as many of us were experiencing with even our closest family and friends! Wings of Hope Living Forward took our great longing to be heard and understood and created events where parents could all come together and meet!

My first retreat was amazing! I made lifelong friends from all walks of life, but we shared the same pain of grief and daily struggles to learn how to live without our precious child!

We all stay in a huge mansion style place, where many of us even share sleeping quarters... We bond, share meals, laugh, and cry together; we hug, love, and support each other! There is a licensed Grief Counselor present for the entire week-long retreat, and she is one of the founders and is amazing!

I am so grateful for this group of parents; together, we save lives and learn how to live again while keeping our Child's spirit alive! Most respectfully,

Client Served

My son was murdered on 02/26/12 by somebody he was helping. He left behind 4 daughters and a son that was yet to be born. My son

Why Me? - Navigating the Unbearable Truth of Grief and Loss

was my life, my only child. We talked every day. When he died part of me died also. Everyone thought I was so brave and so strong, but I just wanted to be with my son. I did not want to live. I met an amazing group of moms who were just like me. They were broken. I was invited to the 1st retreat that is where my healing started. At the retreat, I got to meet face to face other moms. I knew I was no longer alone on this journey. I have formed lifetime friendships with other moms. Now, I am helping other parents who are on this journey. This group has saved my life, and I am trying to give back. Thank you, Shirley, and Renee, you gave me purpose.

Epilogue

In closing, my hope is that you have gained some insight about grief and the places it will take you. Most of all, I hope that through reading my journey, you have discovered that even though you may feel broken, shattered, and at the depths of despair—even wanting to end it all—you can survive the most devastating event that can happen in a parent's life.

I hope you find joy and then choose joy every day. Our lives may now consist of an emptiness, a cloud of sadness that is always lurking, but through it all, we can find grace in our grief. Grief does not define us; rather, it reshapes us, teaching us to live with the pain while still seeking moments of light and love.

May you be reminded that you are not alone in this journey. Whether you are just beginning to navigate your loss or are years into your path, know that healing, however gradual, is possible. The scars remain, but they are a testament to the love we shared and the lives that have forever touched us.

God bless you all, and thank you for reading my book, *Why Me?*

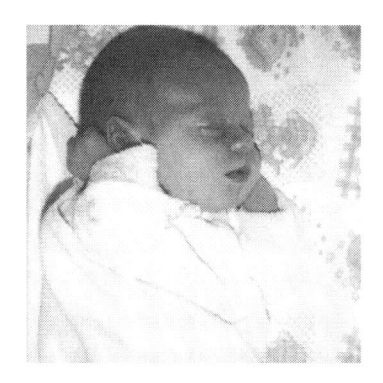

End Notes

If my book "Why Me?" has helped you, send me a note and let me know.

Personal Email: shirleytrippjohnson@gmail.com

Facebook: www.facebook.com/ShirleyTrippJohnson

Closed Facebook Group: **Wings of Hope Living Forward-My Child has Wings**

www.facebook.com/groups/mychildhaswings

Graphics public page: Wings of Hope Living Forward

www.facebook.com/WingsofHopeLivingForward

www.etsy.com/shop/joyinthemourning

Tripp

10/05/82 - 02/17/10

Made in the USA
Columbia, SC
24 February 2025

d80dca72-1fd9-417b-8e40-299540af810aR02